Skillbuilder Workbook
for
**Beebe, Beebe, and Redmond**

# INTERPERSONAL COMMUNICATION
*Relating to Others*

Prepared by
**Kay E. Mueller**
*Iowa State University*

**Allyn and Bacon**
Boston · London · Toronto · Sydney · Tokyo · Singapore

# CONTENTS

**CHAPTER 3**      **Interpersonal Communication and Perception**      41

Objectives
Study Questions
Exercises:

Vocabulary Flash Cards

**PART II      LEARNING INTERPERSONAL COMMUNICATION SKILLS**

**CHAPTER 4**      **Listening and Responding**      63

Objectives
Study Questions
Exercises:

Vocabulary Flash Cards

# PREFACE

This Study Guide contains over 120 activities and exercises designed to help the student understand the principles and develop competency in the use of the communication concepts introduced in *Interpersonal Communication: Relating to Others*. The activities are arranged by chapter so that the student can do the activities outside of class to practice skills and to develop awareness of the concepts as they are introduced in the text and in class.

The exercises in this study guide focus on application and analysis of the concepts discussed in the text. It is important for the student to connect the text information to his or her own life. By doing so, the student can see the relevancy of the material and will be motivated to learn. Most exercises are followed by questions to encourage critical thinking and analysis about the exercise and the application to "real" relationships. The exercises may be required by the instructor to be graded or to stimulate discussion in class. I recommend doing the exercises prior to class discussion of the concepts. This gives the student opportunity to enter discussions with well-prepared examples.

In the attempt to make this study guide "user friendly" for the student, I included Study Questions and Vocabulary Flash Cards for each chapter. The questions serve as a review for each chapter to help the student prepare for tests. The flash cards aid the student in learning the vocabulary words for clear understanding of the communication concepts discussed in class and on tests.

# ACKNOWLEDGEMENTS

I thank Steve Beebe, Susan Beebe, and Mark Redmond for trusting in me to create and organize activities to accompany the excellent, interculturally focused textbook, *Interpersonal Communication: Relating to Others*. It was an honor to be associated with their unique perspective of interpersonal communication.

I enjoyed putting this activity manual together and hope that you as a student have fun with the exercises. As I tell my students, what you get out of your classes is directly related to the effort you put into them. The activities in this guide are designed to help you get some fun out of the concepts you read about in the text. I have tried to include activities that will fit a variety of lifestyles, so there should be some in each chapter that are appropriate for everyone.

I am grateful to Ms. Carla Daves at Allyn and Bacon Publishers for inviting me to write this activity manual and for her patience with my complicated schedule during the creation of this manual.

I must also thank my children--Lauri, Jeff, Jordan, Kristi, Cathy, and David--for contributing ideas for activities and for allowing me to use them as examples during my classroom lectures. Last, but certainly not least, I thank Mark, my husband and best friend, for helping with typing, formatting, and proofing this manual, as well as lots of listening to ideas and understanding my moods during this project and every day of my life.

# CHAPTER 1
# INTRODUCTION TO INTERPERSONAL COMMUNICATION

## OBJECTIVES

After studying the material in this chapter of *Interpersonal Communication: Relating to Others* and completing the exercises in this section of the study guide, you should understand:

1. the difference between the definitions of communication, human communication, and interpersonal communication,
2. communication as action, interaction, and transaction,
3. the three principles of communication,
4. the key components of the communication process,
5. the three goals of communication,
6. why it is useful to study interpersonal communication,
7. the seven characteristics of interpersonal relationships, and
8. the strategies which can improve your communication effectiveness.

## STUDY QUESTIONS

You should be able to answer the following questions:

1. What is the difference in communication, human communication, and interpersonal communication?
2. What is meant by human communication as action, interaction, and transaction?
3. What are the four principles of interpersonal communication?
4. What does it mean to say that language is "a system of symbols?"
5. What are the five contexts in which we communicate?
6. What are the three goals for interpersonal communication?
7. What are the four reasons we should study interpersonal communication?
8. What are the characteristics of interpersonal relationships?
9. How can you improve your interpersonal communication?
10. What is the difference between decentering and empathizing?

## EXERCISE 1.1   IDENTIFYING THE "PEOPLE" INVOLVED IN YOUR COMMUNICATION EVENTS

**Purposes:**
1. To understand the complexity of everyday communication.
2. To recognize your contribution to communication exchanges
3. To help you realize how you communicate differently with various people.

**Directions:**
1. List four people with whom you communicate on a daily basis.
2. Identify your relationship with each person (friend, son/daughter, roommate, etc.).
3. Describe a typical conversation with each person (what you talk about--topics, how each of you talk--tone of voice, amount of information shared, length of conversations, etc.)


PERSON #1

   Relationship: _____

   Description of conversation: _____

   _____

   _____

   _____

   _____


PERSON #2

   Relationship: _____

   Description of conversation: _____

   _____

   _____

   _____

   _____

PERSON #3

    Relationship: _____

    Description of conversation: _____

    _____

    _____

    _____

    _____


PERSON #4

    Relationship: _____

    Description of conversation: _____

    _____

    _____

    _____

    _____


**Questions:**

1.    What are the differences between each of your conversations?


2.    How are the conversations the same?


3.    What did you contribute to each of the conversations?

**EXERCISE 1.2     RECOGNIZING COMMUNICATION AS A SET OF SYMBOLS**

**Purposes:**
1.     To understand that language is a set of symbols used to create meaning.

**Directions:**
1.     Identify symbols (emblems) for examples in each of the categories listed below.
2.     List specific examples to illustrate each category.
2.     Draw or write the standard symbol that identifies each example.

PROFESSIONS                    SYMBOL OR EMBLEM

GANGS                          SYMBOL OR EMBLEM

ROCK BANDS                     SYMBOL OR EMBLEM

CORPORATIONS                   SYMBOL OR EMBLEM

# EXERCISE 1.3     REALIZING YOUR COMMUNICATION STRENGTHS AND WEAKNESSES

## Purposes:
1.      To recognize your strong areas of communication.
2.      To recognize areas of communication in which you need to improve.
3.      To understand how you become aware on your interpersonal communication strengths and your areas that need improvement.

## Directions:
1.      List three of your interpersonal communication strengths.
2.      List three interpersonal communication areas that you think need the most improvement.


STRENGTHS

1._____

2._____

3._____


AREAS TO IMPROVE

1._____

2._____

3._____


## Questions:
1.      How do you know you have these strengths?  What kind of feedback do you get from others?  How have your experiences with others confirmed that you do these things well?
2.      How do you know you need to improve in these areas?  What kind of feedback do you get from others?  How have your experiences with others confirmed that you need to work on these areas?

## EXERCISE 1.4    ASSESSING YOUR INTERPERSONAL RELATIONSHIPS

**Purposes:**
1.    To understand how communication events are guided by the context in which the event occurs.
2.    To understand how each of the five contexts (psychological, relational, situational, environmental, and cultural) affects the individuals in a relationship differently.
3.    To determine the degree of interpersonalness of your relationships.

**Directions:**
1.    Select three relationships to assess (work, school, friendship, family, roommate, or romantic).

First relational partner _____

Second relational partner _____

Third relational partner _____

2.    For each relationship, complete the items below using the following scale:

> 5 - Definitely true
> 4 - Mostly true
> 3 - Neither true nor false
> 2 - Mostly false
> 1 - Definitely false

| | RELATIONSHIPS | | |
|---|:---:|:---:|:---:|
| | 1 | 2 | 3 |
| 1.    My partner and I use psychological information exclusively as the basis for predicting each other's responses. | ___ | ___ | ___ |
| 2.    I have a high degree of trust and a positive history with my partner. | ___ | ___ | ___ |
| 3.    Most of the rules we use for communicating in our relationship are unique to our relationship. | ___ | ___ | ___ |
| 4.    Our roles in the relationship are defined almost exclusively by our individual characteristics. | ___ | ___ | ___ |
| 5.    Our goals for communicating include the satisfaction of both personal and mutual needs. | ___ | ___ | ___ |
| TOTAL | ___ | ___ | ___ |

The possible range of your scores is 4 to 25, indicating degrees of interpersonalness. Scores of 15 and lower lean toward noninterpersonal, while scores of 16 and higher lean toward interpersonal.

**Questions:**

1.  Is one of your relationships more interpersonal than the others? In what ways?

    _____

    _____

2.  How do your relationships differ on each of the five dimensions of interpersonal communication? What does this indicate about your relationships?

    _____

    _____

    _____

3.  How does the other person's cultural background affect how she or he responds to you and your messages?

    _____

    _____

4.  How do the situation and the environment affect how you and your partner communicate your messages?

    _____

    _____

5.  How does the content and/or the way the messages are communicated change due to the place and the surroundings in which you are communicating?

    _____

    _____

(Adapted from: Berko, R. M., Rosenfeld, L. B., & Samovar, L. A. (1994). *Connecting: A Culture-Sensitive Approach to Interpersonal Communication Competency.* Orlando, FL: Harcourt Brace.)

## EXERCISE 1.5    UNDERSTANDING YOUR ETHICAL COMMUNICATION

### Purposes:
1.    To understand the attributes of ethical interpersonal communication.
2.    To become aware of your communication patterns in relation to ethical communication as described in Chapter 1 of the *Interpersonal Communication: Relating to Others.*

### Directions:
1.    Identify three people with whom you communicate on a daily basis.
2.    Evaluate your conversations with these three people over a two day period.
3.    Summarize your findings by filling in the following chart:
For other-orientation, honesty, and keeping confidences rate your conversations according to the scale:

> 5 - always
> 4 - almost always
> 3 - sometimes
> 2 - almost never
> 1 - never

| PERSON | RELATIONSHIP | OTHER-ORIENTATION | HONESTY | KEEP CONFIDENCES |
|---|---|---|---|---|
|  |  |  |  |  |
|  |  |  |  |  |
|  |  |  |  |  |

The higher your score is, the higher your ethical communication behavior is.  Compare your scores between the different people you chose.

### Questions:

1.    How is your ethical behavior the same with all three people?

2.    How is it different?

3.    Why might your ethical communication behavior change, depending on the person and the relationship you have with that person?

8

## EXERCISE 1.6    IMPROVING YOUR RELATIONSHIPS

**Purposes:**
1.    To become aware of how we communicate in a variety of relationships.
2.    To recognize ways we can improve our relationships by changing our communication behavior.

**Directions:**
1.    Identify three people with whom you interact regularly--a family member, a friend, and a co-worker or classmate.
2.    List your positive communication behaviors with each person.
3.    List communication behaviors that create problems with each person.
4.    List ways you could change your communication behaviors to improve the relationship you have with each person.


FAMILY MEMBER'S NAME: _____

    Positive Behaviors:    _____

    _____

    Problematic Behaviors:_____

    _____

    Ways to Improve:    _____

    _____

    _____


FRIEND'S NAME:    _____

    Positive Behaviors:    _____

    _____

    Problematic Behaviors:_____

    _____

    Ways to Improve:    _____

    _____

CO-WORKER/CLASSMATE'S NAME: _____

    Positive Behaviors: _____

                                 _____

    Problematic Behaviors:_____

                                 _____

    Ways to Improve: _____

                                 _____

# EXERCISE 1.7     IDENTIFYING YOUR COMMUNICATION RULES

## Purposes:
1.      To become aware of your personal communication rules that you expect others to follow.
2.      To understand the difference between explicit and implicit communication rules.
3.      To recognize how you react when your communication rules are violated.
4.      To determine how you developed your communication rules.

## Directions:
1.      List five rules you have which govern your communication interactions with others.
2.      Identify how many of the rules you have verbalized to other people with whom you communicate.
3.      List the ways you react when someone violates your communication rules.
4.      For each rule, state how you learned the expected behaviors.

| RULES | VERBALIZED | UNVERBALIZED | REACTION | ORIGIN |
|-------|-----------|--------------|----------|--------|
|       |           |              |          |        |
|       |           |              |          |        |
|       |           |              |          |        |
|       |           |              |          |        |
|       |           |              |          |        |

| Communication | Human Communication |
|---|---|
| Interpersonal Communication | Encode |
| Decode | Receiver |
| Message | Channel |
| Noise | Context |
| Feedback | Episode |
| Symbol | Interpersonal Relationship |

| | |
|---|---|
| The process of making sense out of the world and attempting to share that sense with others. | The process of acting upon information. |
| To translate ideas, feelings and thoughts into a code. | The process of interacting simultaneously and sharing mutual influence with another person. |
| The person who decodes a message and attempts to make sense out of what the source has encoded. | To interpret ideas, feelings, and thoughts that have been traslated into a code. |
| The pathway through which messages are sent. | The written, spoken and unspoken elements of communication to which people assign meaning. |
| The physical and psychologic communication environment | Information, either literal or psychological, that interferes with the accuracy to the reception of a communication of a message. |
| A sequence of interaction between individuals during which the message of one person influences the message of another | The response to a message. |
| The connections we forge with another human being through interpersonal communication. | A representation of something else. |

| | |
|---|---|
| Cultural Information | Sociological Information |
| Psychological Information | Bonding |
| Psychological Context | Relational Context |
| Situational Context | Environmental Context |
| Cultural Context | Decentering |
| Empathy | |

| | |
|---|---|
| Information based upon what we know about another person's membership in certain groups. | Information about language and dominant values learned in a given culture that we assume someone shares even if we know little about him or her. |
| The process of emotionally and psychologically becoming attached or enmeshed with another person. | Information about the unique person with whom we are interacting. |
| All those factors that evolve when two people meet and continue a relationship; level of trust, degree of self-disclosure; level of power and control, and the history of the relationship. | Elements that an individual brings to a relationship, including needs, desires, values, personality, and self-concept. |
| The physical surroundings in which people communicate. | The event or reason two people are communication with one another. |
| The process of thinking about anothers person's thoughts and feelings. | All elements within a culture such as learned rules, behaviors and values, that affect the interaction. |
| | The ability to "feel for" another person, or to "stand inside another's shoes." |

# CHAPTER 2
# COMMUNICATION AND SELF

## OBJECTIVES

After studying the material in this chapter of *Interpersonal Communication: Relating to Others* and completing the exercises in this section of the study guide, you should understand:

1. the difference between self-concept and self-esteem,
2. how your attitudes, beliefs, and values shape your behavior and self-image,
3. the different dimensions of self,
4. how self-concept is developed through interaction with others, association with groups, the roles we assume, and self labels,
5. how self-concept affects your relationships with others,
6. how you communication style affects your relationships with others, and
7. how to improve your self-esteem.

## STUDY QUESTIONS

You should be able to answer the following questions:

1. What is the difference between self-concept and self-esteem?
2. What are attitudes, beliefs, and values, and how are they related to self-concept?
3. What are the three dimensions of self?
4. What are the four factors that contribute to the development of self-concept?
5. What is the process of decentering and how does it relate to sense of self?
6. How does self-concept and self-esteem affect interpersonal communication and relationships?
7. What is the self-fulfilling prophecy?
8. What are the four primary communication styles that impact the way we deliver messages?
9. Define and explain each of the strategies for improving your self-esteem?

# EXERCISE 2.1     IDENTIFYING YOUR "SELVES"

**Purpose:**
1.     To understand yourself in three ways:
       a.     How you see yourself (perceived self)
       b.     How you want to be (desired self)
       c.     How others see you (presenting self)

**Directions:**
1.     List your favorite animal or bird.  Write three characteristics of that animal that you admire.
2.     List your second favorite animal or bird.  Write three characteristics of that animal that you admire.
3.     List your third favorite animal or bird.  Write three characteristics of that animal that you admire.

| Animal | Characteristic 1 | Characteristic 2 | Characteristic 3 |
|---|---|---|---|
| 1. | | | |
| 2. | | | |
| 3. | | | |

**Explanation:**
Animal #1 represents how you would like to be or your desired self.
Animal #2 represents how you are or your perceived self.
Animal #3 represents how others see you or your presenting self.

This would be a fun exercise to do at a party.  Share this with three friends to find out if your perceptions of yourself agree with theirs and if your perceptions of them agree with their perception of themselves.

**Questions:**
1.     With which characteristics that you identified for each "self" did you agree? With what characteristics did you disagree?  Why or why not?
2.     With which characteristics of you did your friends agree?  With which did they disagree?  Why or why not?
3.     With which characteristics did your friends agree about themselves?  With which did they disagree?  Why or why not?
4.     Which characteristics of your friends did you agree with about them?  With which did you disagree?  Why or why not?

# EXERCISE 2.2    SEEING A VARIETY OF ASPECTS OF YOURSELF

## Purpose:

1.    To become aware of your abilities, attitudes, possessions, accomplishments that are part of your self-concept.

## Directions:

1.    Draw a coat of arms with eight panels.
2.    On the front of the coat-of-arms draw figures or pictures to represent each of the following questions:

    A.    What is something at which you are very good and enjoy doing?

    B.    What is something you are working to be better at or trying to improve?

    C.    What is something with which you constantly struggle?

    D.    What is your most prized possession--something purchased, earned, created by you, or given to you?

    E.    What was your greatest accomplishment in the past year?

    F.    What was the greatest setback for you in the past year?

    G.    If you were given only one year to live and you were guaranteed success, what would you do?

    H.    On your tombstone, what three words would you have inscribed that best describes you?

## EXERCISE 2.3    FINDING YOUR UNIQUENESS

**Purpose:**
1.    To help you realize the qualities you possess that make you who you are.

**Directions:**
1.    Think about each of the following questions.
2.    Write down your initial impressions or thoughts for each question.  BE
      HONEST!!

---

1.    Write three positive words that describe you.

      (10) _____ (2) _____ (3) _____

2.    What single factor contributes most to your self-esteem?  Why?

      _____

      _____

      _____

3.    What do you consider to be your greatest accomplishment?  Why?

      _____

      _____

      _____

4.    What would your best friend say is your most positive attribute?  Why?

      _____

      _____

      _____

5.   What was the most positive message your parents gave you? Why?

_____

_____

_____

6.   What would you most like to be remembered for in your life? Why?

_____

_____

_____

7.   Circle the words that you believe *best* describe your character, talents, and appearance.

| | | | |
|---|---|---|---|
| talented | motivated | humorous | outgoing |
| creative | responsible | organized | reserved |
| caring | professional | understanding | athletic |
| mature | technical | attractive | a leader |

8.   List briefly what you are most proud of:

- a difficult job _____
- a goal you reached _____
- an award you received _____
- a compliment you gave _____
- a compliment you received _____
- a habit you changed _____

(Adapted from Palladino, C. D. (1994) *Developing Self-esteem: A Guide for Positive Success.* Menlo Park, CA: Crisp.)

## EXERCISE 2.4    IDENTIFYING HOW YOU BECAME YOU

**Purposes:**
1.    To understand how you developed your view of who you are.
2.    To understand how your view of yourself affects the way you communicate with others.

**Directions:**
1.    Make a list of ten words or descriptions that you have heard others use to describe you in the last month.
2.    Identify who described you in that way.
3.    Record how many times each person described you in each way.
4.    Record the relationship to you or title of the person(s) who made the descriptions.
5.    State how the descriptions impact your communication with the others.

Description          Person(s)          # of times          Relationship

_____

_____

_____

_____

_____

**Questions:**

1.    How is your communication behavior different with the people who described
      you?

      _____

      _____

2.    Which descriptions do you view as positive influence on your self-concept?

      _____

      _____

3.    Which are negative influences?

      _____

## EXERCISE 2.5    GIVING YOURSELF LABELS

**Purpose:**
1.    To help you recognize the skills, talents, and virtues that make up your self-concept.

**Directions:**
1.    Write an ad for the DateMate section of a newspaper or (if you are attached) an application for a Beauty or Talent show.
2.    Use as many descriptive adjectives as you can think of to represent your personality, character, and appearance.

Have a close friend or family member write another ad or application for you. Compare the descriptions of each list of adjectives.

**Questions:**
1.    What are the similarities and the differences between the lists?

2.    How do the labels you gave yourself compare to the list of Stereotypical Labels for Males and Females in *Interpersonal Communication: Relating to Others?*

3.    How do the labels your partner gave to you compare to the list of Stereotypical Labels for Males and Females in *Interpersonal Communication: Relating to Others?*

**EXERCISE 2.6**     **LEARNING TO "BRAG" ABOUT YOURSELF**

**Purpose:**
1.     To recognize your sense of self-worth.

**Directions:**
1.     Make a list of twenty positives about yourself--possessions, talents, abilities, accomplishments.
2.     Share three of your brags to three different people. (I have ---, I am good at ---, I can do --- well, I did ---).

YOUR "BRAGS"

1. _____

2. _____

3. _____

4. _____

5. _____

6. _____

7. _____

8. _____

9. _____

10. _____

11. _____

12. _____

13. _____

14. _____

15. _____

16. _____

17. _____

18. _____

19. _____

20. _____

## Questions:

1.  How did you feel bragging about yourself?

    _____

    _____

    _____

2.  What are the consequences of thinking positive thoughts versus thinking negative thoughts about your self when you communicate to others?

    _____

    _____

    _____

3.  How does positive thinking effect your self-concept?

    _____

    _____

    _____

# EXERCISE 2.7      HELPING OTHERS DEVELOP POSITIVE SELF IMAGES

## Purposes:
1.      To understand the impact positive comments can have on the self image of others.
2.      To understand how you can help shape the image of another's self.

## Directions:
1.      On a sheet of paper, list the names of your family members.
2.      Leave a space between each name.  In that space write down the nicest thing you can say about each of your family members.
3.      Give each member a copy of your comments about him/her.
4.      Observe the reaction of each person upon receiving his/her message.
         (You could also do this exercise with roommates or friends.)

NAMES OF FAMILY MEMBERS (FRIENDS)

1.      _____

Comment:      _____

                   _____

2.      _____

Comment:      _____

                   _____

3.      _____

Comment:      _____

                   _____

4.      _____

Comment:      _____

                   _____

5.      _____

Comment:      _____

                   _____

6. _____

Comment: _____

_____

**Questions:**

1. How difficult or easy was it to say nice things about your family members? Why or why not?

   _____

   _____

2. Who was the easiest person to share a positive message with? Why?

   _____

   _____

3. Who was the most difficult person to share a positive message with? Why?

   _____

   _____

4. How did each person react to the positive message you shared with him/her?

   _____

   _____

   _____

   _____

   _____

   _____

**EXERCISE 2.8**     **RECOGNIZING CHANGES IN YOUR SELF**

**Purposes:**
1.     To realize that your view of your self changes over time.
2.     To understand why your self has changes.

**Directions:**
1.     Identify two components of your self-concept that have changed in the last year or two.
2.     Identify two components of your self-concept that you have discovered about yourself in the last year or two.
3.     Identify how you became aware of the recently changed or discovered components of your self.
4.     Identify how interpersonal interactions might have influenced the changes and/or the discoveries.

**CHANGED SELF**

1.     _____ ____

       _____

       What made you realize there was a change? _____

       _____

       _____

       How did interpersonal interactions influence the change?     _____

       _____

       _____

2.     _____ ____

       _____

       What made you realize there was a change? _____

       _____

       _____

How did interpersonal interactions influence the change? _____

_____

_____


## NEWLY DISCOVERED SELF

1. _____

   _____

   How did you discover this difference? _____

   _____

   _____

   How did interpersonal interactions influence the discovery? _____

   _____

   _____


2. _____

   _____

   How did you discover this difference? _____

   _____

   _____

   How did interpersonal interactions influence the discovery? _____

   _____

   _____

# EXERCISE 2.9    RECOGNIZING THE IMPACT OF "SELF TALK"

## Purposes:
1.    To recognize self talk in others.
2.    To understand the affect self talk has on a person's attitude and behavior.

## Directions:
1.    Watch a television sit-com or soap opera ("Days of our Lives" is particularly good for this exercise).
2.    Observe the way the actors talk to themselves about different situations.
3.    Distinguish between the positive and the negative messages.
4.    Analyze the impact of the self talk on the behavior of the actors.

POSITIVE MESSAGES GIVEN:

NEGATIVE MESSAGES GIVEN:

## Questions:

1.    How did the messages the actors gave themselves impact their behavior?

_____

_____

_____

2.    How are the messages the actors give to themselves the same or different from the messages you give to yourself.

_____

_____

_____

# EXERCISE 2.10   WEARING MANY HATS

## Purposes:
1.  To realize the number of different roles you perform in one day.
2.  To become aware of your communication behavior in different roles.
3.  To understand the influence of gender on roles you perform.

## Directions:
1.  List all the roles you performed during one day in the last week.
2.  Identify the expected behavior for you in each of your roles.
3.  Analyze how your expectations developed.
4.  Analyze how your communication behavior is the same or different in the roles.

| Roles | Behaviors Expected | Where expectations came from | Communication Behavior |
|-------|--------------------|-----------------------------|------------------------|
|       |                    |                             |                        |
|       |                    |                             |                        |
|       |                    |                             |                        |
|       |                    |                             |                        |
|       |                    |                             |                        |
|       |                    |                             |                        |
|       |                    |                             |                        |
|       |                    |                             |                        |
|       |                    |                             |                        |

## Questions:

1.  Which of your roles are influenced by gender stereotypes?

2.  How do these gender stereotypical role expectations affect your interactions with others?

# EXERCISE 2.11     DISCOVERING IMPACTS ON YOUR SELF-ESTEEM

## Purposes:

1. To understand who and/or what impacts the positive and negative views you have about yourself.
2. To realize the ways others impact your self and why.

## Directions:

### POSITIVE IMPACT

1. List three people, events, accomplishments, etc. that make a positive impact on your self-concept.
2. State what each of these people do or what happened during an event to make the positive impact.

| WHAT/WHO | HOW/WHY |
|----------|---------|
| 1. | |
| 2. | |
| 3. | |

How you can INCREASE OR MAINTAIN the positive impact:

_____

### NEGATIVE IMPACT

1. List three people, events, accomplishments, etc. that make a negative impact on your self-concept.
2. State what each of these people do or what happened during an event to make the negative impact.

| WHO/WHAT | HOW/WHY |
|----------|---------|
| 1. | |
| 2. | |
| 3. | |

How you can DECREASE the negative impact

_____

## EXERCISE 2.12    CHANGING NEGATIVE MESSAGES INTO POSITIVE

**Purpose:**

1.     To learn to turn negative messages positive messages.

**Directions:**

1.     List five negative messages that you either remember receiving as a child or messages that you hear currently. An example might be: "You are just a pesky, tagalong brat."

---

1.

2.

3.

4.

5.

Now turn these same five negative messages into positive ones by putting the statement in the first person (I or my), using the present tense, and/or stating what you want. Example: "I learned valuable lessons by being with my brother/sister."

1.

2.

3.

4.

5.

Put all five of your positive statements on 3x5 cards and keep in a place you can see them daily. Any time you hear a negative message, turn it into a positive message in the same way and put it on a 3x5 card to add to your collection of positive self-esteem builders.

**EXERCISE 2.13     ENJOYING YOURSELF**

**Purpose:**
1.     To help you understand how the activities in which you participate effect your image of yourself.

**Directions:**
1.     List 20 THINGS that you enjoy doing. These activities may be hobbies, amusement, classes, sports, or social activities.

ACTIVITY                ALONE OR WITH OTHERS                SKILLS USED

1.

2.

3.

4.

5.

6.

7.

8.

9.

10.

11.

12.

13.

14.

15.

16.

17.

18.

19.

20.

**Questions:**

1.  Are there any significant patterns that have an impact on or form your "self?"

    _____

    _____

    _____

2.  How pleased are you with the amount of interaction you have with others when you do these activities?

    _____

    _____

    _____

3.  How pleased are you with the number of different skills you are using?

    _____

    _____

    _____

4.  What can you do to add variety to the things you enjoy doing?

    _____

    _____

    _____

| | |
|---|---|
| Self | Self-Concept |
| Attitudes | Beliefs |
| Values | Material Self |
| Social Self | Spiritual Self |
| Looking Glass Self | Androgynous Role |
| Self-reflexiveness | Self-esteem |
| Life Positions | Specific-Other Perspective |

| | |
|---|---|
| A person's subjective description of who he or she is. | The sum total of who a person is; a person's central inner force. |
| The ways in which you structure your understanding of reality--what is true and what is false. | Learned predispositions to respond to a person, object, or idea in a favorable or unfavorable way. |
| Your concept of self as reflected in a total of all of the tangible things you own. | Enduring concepts of good and bad, right and wrong. |
| Your concept of self based upon your thoughts and introspection about your values and moral standards. | Your concept of self as developed through your personal, social interactions with others. |
| A gender role that includes both masculine and feminine qualities. | A concept that suggests we learn who we are based upon our interactions with others that are reflected back to us. |
| Your evaluation of your worth or value as reflected in your perception of such things as your skills, abilities, talents, and appearance. | The human ability to think about what we are doing while we are doing it. |
| The process of relying upon information that a person observes or imagines about another person that is used to predict a person's behavior. | Your feeling of being either "OK" or "Not OK" as reflected in your sense of worth and self esteem. |

| | |
|---|---|
| Generalized-Other Perspective | Self-Fulfilling Prophesy |
| Selective Exposure | Communication Style (Social Style) |
| Assertiveness | Responsiveness |
| Driver Style | Analytical Style |
| Expressive Style | Amiable Style |
| Back-Up Communication Style | Intrapersonal Communication |
| Visualization | Reframing |

| | |
|---|---|
| The notion that predictions about your future actions are likely to come true because you believe that they will come true. | The process of relying upon information about many people or people in general that is observed or imagined that is used to predict a person's behavior. |
| Your consistent way of relating to others based upon your personality, self concept and self esteem. | A principle that suggests we tend to place ourselves in situations that are consistent with our self concept and self esteem. |
| A dimension of the Wilson Learning social sytle model that describes a person quality of placing the feeling sof others above our own and expressing those feelings. | A dimension of the Wilson Learning social style model that describes a personal quality that refers to an individuals effort to control others. |
| A communication style characterized by high assertiveness and low expressiveness, considerable attention to detail and task achievement. | A communication style characterized by high achievement, assertiveness, and controlled emotions. |
| A communication style characterized by high degree of expressiveness and sensitivity toward others and a minimum of assertiveness. | A communication style characterized by a high degree of expressiveness and assertiveness; there is a tendency to both control others and to respond emotionally or impulsively. |
| Communication within yourself that includes your self talk. | The communication style we often use when we are under stress or when our primary style does not achieve the desired results. |
| The process of redefining events and experience from a different point of view. | A technique of imagining that you are performing a particular task in a certain way. Positive visualization can enhance your self esteem |

# CHAPTER 3
# INTERPERSONAL COMMUNICATION AND PERCEPTION

## OBJECTIVES

After studying the material in this chapter of *Interpersonal Communication: Relating to Others* and completing the exercises in this section of the study guide, you should understand:

1. the definitions of perception and interpersonal perception,
2. the three stages of interpersonal perception,
3. how interpersonal perception is related to interpersonal communication,
4. the processes of impression formation, implicit personality theory, attribution theory, and constructs,
5. the ten factors which distort the accuracy of our interpersonal perceptions, and
6. how to improve you interpersonal perceptions.

## STUDY QUESTIONS

You should be able to answer the following questions:

1. What is the definition of perception and interpersonal perception?
2. What are the three stages of interpersonal perception and what happens in each stage?
3. What does it mean to punctuate information as we organize it?
4. What is the difference between passive perception and active perception?
5. How do the primacy effect and the recency effect relate to impression formation?
6. How does the implicit personality theory relate to interpersonal perception?
7. What is the purpose of organizing perceptions through personal constructs?
8. How do the Correspondent Inference Theory and the Causal Attribution Theory relate to the attributing meaning to behavior?
9. What are the barriers to making accurate perceptions?
10. How can you improve your ability to make accurate interpersonal perceptions?

# EXERCISE 3.1        CATEGORIZING OTHERS BY LIKES AND DISLIKES

## Purpose:
1.    To become aware of how you perceive people differently because of your attraction level to them.

## Directions:
1.    Make a list of five people that you like.
2.    Write down as many personal characteristics and qualities as you can think of about each person.
3.    Make a list of five people that you don't like.
4.    Write down as many personal characteristics and qualities as you can think of about each person.

PEOPLE YOU LIKE                              CHARACTERISTICS

1.    _____          _____

                                  _____

                                  _____

                                  _____

                                  _____

2.    _____          _____

                                  _____

                                  _____

                                  _____

                                  _____

3.    _____          _____

                                  _____

                                  _____

                                  _____

                                  _____

4. _____     _____

_____

_____

_____

_____

5. _____     _____

_____

_____

_____

_____

PEOPLE YOU DON'T LIKE     CHARACTERISTICS

1. _____     _____

_____

_____

_____

_____

2. _____     _____

_____

_____

_____

_____

3. _____     _____

                           _____

                           _____

                           _____

                           _____

4. _____     _____

                           _____

                           _____

                           _____

                           _____

5. _____     _____

                           _____

                           _____

                           _____

**Questions:**

1.  When comparing the lists, what positive (complimentary) characteristics did you have?

    _____

2.  Which list had the most positive characteristics? Why do you think that happened?

    _____

3.  What negative (uncomplimentary) characteristics did you observe?

    _____

4.  Which had the most negative qualities? Why do you think that happened?

    _____

## EXERCISE 3.2    FILLING IN THE GAPS

**Purpose:**
1.    To realize how you often structure information by filling in the gaps.

**Directions:**
1.    Walk through a large parking lot and watch cars on the road.
2.    Look for personalized license plates that appear to have meaning to the owner.
3.    Try to create familiar words from the meaningless group of letters and numbers that could lead to a conclusion about the car owner.  (Example: XSPAR10 = ex-Spartan = Michigan State University alumnus)

LICENSE PLATE          MEANING          CONCLUSION


## EXERCISE 3.3    EXAMINING RELATIONSHIPS AND PERCEPTION

**Purposes:**
1.    To become aware of the different views two people have of each other.
2.    To investigate the affect of perception accuracy on relationship levels.

**Directions:**
1.    Choose a significant other with whom you communicate frequently.  Write down a description of yourself and of your friend.  Have your friend write down a description of you and of him/herself.  Compare your descriptions of each other.  Check the accuracy of  both perceptions.

2.    Choose a casual friend with whom you communicate once in a while.  Write down a description of  yourself and of your friend.  Have your friend write down a description of you and of him/herself.  Compare your descriptions of each other.  Check the accuracy of both perceptions.

3.    Choose a new acquaintance with whom you communicate very little.  Write down a description of yourself and of your friend.  Have your friend write down a description of you and of him/herself.  Compare your descriptions of each other.  Check the accuracy of both perceptions.

**Questions:**
1.    What were the differences in accuracy between the three friends?
2.    How did the level of the relationships affect the accuracy of perceptions of each other?

**EXERCISE 3.4    SEEING IS BELIEVING--WHO'S RIGHT?**

**Purpose:**
1.    To understand how different people see situations differently.

**Directions:**
1.    Attend a social event (party, dinner at a restaurant, game, concert, political rally, etc.).
2.    Interview three people who also attended the event.  Ask them questions about their views regarding the event.  (What did they like/dislike?  Most interesting/least interesting aspect?)

EVENT:        _____

        PERSON #1    _____

            Opinion        _____

                        _____

        PERSON # 2    _____

            Opinion        _____

                        _____

        PERSON #3    _____

            Opinion        _____

                        _____

**Questions;**

1.    What similarities were there in the perceptions?  Why do you think these people saw the event in these same ways?

2.    What differences were there in the perceptions?  Why do you think these people saw the event in different ways?

## EXERCISE 3.5     CHANGING FIRST IMPRESSIONS

**Purposes:**
1.     To help you understand the impact of a first impression.
2.     To help you realize what it takes to change an impression.

**Directions:**
1.     Think of your three best friends.
2.     Write down what you thought of each person when you met him/her.
3.     Write down what you think of each person now--why is he/she still your friend?
4.     Write down what influenced any changes in your thoughts about each person from the first meeting to now.

FRIEND     FIRST IMPRESSION          CURRENT IMPRESSION     CHANGES

_____

_____

_____

**Questions:**

1.     How did your impressions change about your friends?

    _____

2.     How many of your first impressions were negative?  Positive?

    _____

3.     How long did it take to change the negative impressions?

    _____

4.     What made you change your impressions?

    _____

## EXERCISE 3.6     EXPLAINING WHY PEOPLE DO WHAT THEY DO

**Purposes:**
1.  To understand the interpretations you make about others' behavior.
2.  To practice explaining behavior through intentionality, circumstance, stimulus, and person.

**Directions:**
1.  For the next few days, observe three people and record your interpretations of their behavior in a specific situation.
2.  After recording the information, explain possible intentionality or unintentionality of the behavior.
3.  Explain the possible causes for the each person's behavior due to circumstance, stimulus, and person.

*PERSON #1*

Describe behavior: _____ _____

_____

Give a possible intentional explanation for the behavior: _____

_____

Give a possible unintentional explanation for the behavior: _____

_____

State a possible circumstantial cause for the behavior: _____

_____

State a possible stimulus (external) cause for the behavior: _____

_____

State a possible person (internal) cause for the behavior: _____

_____

**PERSON #2**
Describe behavior: _____ _____

_____

Give a possible intentional explanation for the behavior: _____

_____

Give a possible unintentional explanation for the behavior: _____

_____

State a possible circumstantial cause for the behavior: _____

_____

State a possible stimulus (external) cause for the behavior: _____

_____

State a possible person (internal) cause for the behavior: _____

_____

**PERSON #3**
Describe behavior: _____ _____

_____

Give a possible intentional explanation for the behavior: _____

_____

Give a possible unintentional explanation for the behavior: _____

_____

State a possible circumstantial cause for the behavior: _____

_____

State a possible stimulus (external) cause for the behavior: _____

_____

State a possible person (internal) cause for the behavior: _____

_____

# EXERCISE 3.7    CREATING A PERCEPTION JOURNAL

## Purpose:
1.    To realize the impact that perceptions have on communication behavior.

## Directions:
1.    Over the next few days observe the interpersonal interactions that you have with four different individuals.
2.    Record your observations of the behavior of each person.
3.    Give your interpretation or attribution of meaning to each of the behaviors.
4.    Explain how your interpretation affected your behavior toward the other person.
5.    After the interaction has ended, ask the other person to explain their behavior or to explain what meaning they intended by their behavior.

| OBSERVATION | INTERPRETATION | AFFECT ON MY BEHAVIOR | OTHER'S EXPLANATION |
|---|---|---|---|
| My roommate came in, slamming things around the room, swearing, and scowling. | My roommate was angry at me for leaving stuff on the floor. | I got mad and started to call my roommate names and walked out of the place. | When I came back, I asked my roommate why he/she was angry. It was because he/she just flunked a test and he/she was worried about staying on the Dean's List. |

_____

_____


_____

## Questions:

1.      Which perceptions were most correct?

   _____

   _____


2.      What is your relationship to the person(s) that you were able to accurately perceive their behavior? Why do you think relationship contributed to your accuracy?

   _____

   _____


3.      What is your relationship to the person(s) that you had the most difficulty making accurate perceptions of behavior? Why do you think relationship contributed to your inaccuracy?

   _____

   _____

# EXERCISE 3.8     CHECKING YOUR PERCEPTIONS

## Purpose:
1.    To practice checking on the accuracy of your perceptions in your interpersonal interactions.

## Directions:
1.    In three different interpersonal interactions you have in the next few days, observe behaviors that confuse you or where the meaning of the behavior is not clear to you. Try to include at least one person from a different cultural background than yours.
2.    Make an interpretation of each of the behaviors.
3.    Practice using indirect perception checking to determine if your interpretation of the behavior is correct or not by paying closer attention to the other person's voice, words, and body movements.
4.    To increase your accuracy, practice using direct perception checking by telling the other person what behaviors you are observing, what the behaviors mean to you, and then asking for confirmation of your interpretation.
5.    Record a brief description of the interactions below, explaining the behaviors, your interpretations, what you focused on indirectly, and how you asked for confirmation directly.

PERSON #1

Description of the interaction: _____

Explanation of the behavior: _____

_____

Your meaning: _____

_____

What you focused on indirectly: _____

_____

How you checked your accuracy: _____

_____

PERSON #2

Description of the interaction:_____

Explanation of the behavior: _____

_____

Your meaning: _____

_____

What you focused on indirectly: _____

_____

How you checked your accuracy: _____

_____

PERSON #2

Description of the interaction:_____

Explanation of the behavior: _____

_____

Your meaning: _____

_____

What you focused on indirectly: _____

_____

How you checked your accuracy: _____

_____

## Questions:

1. In which situations were your perceptions most accurate?

_____

2. What information helped you make perceptions most accurately?

_____

_____

**EXERCISE 3.9      FOCUSING ON THE OBVIOUS**

**Purposes:**
1.   To become aware of the type of information you take in when meeting new people.
2.   To understand how you structure information by categories such as physical, role, psychological, and social behavior.

**Directions:**
1.   Observe 10 strangers whom you encounter on campus, in town, or at a Mall.
2.   Write down your first impression of each person.
3.   List the information that led to your impression of each.

| PERSON | IMPRESSION | INFORMATION USED |
|---|---|---|
|  |  |  |
|  |  |  |
|  |  |  |
|  |  |  |
|  |  |  |

|  |  |  |
|---|---|---|
|  |  |  |
|  |  |  |
|  |  |  |
|  |  |  |

**Questions:**

1.    What information did you use frequently for your impressions?

    _____

    _____

2.    What information was not used frequently?

    _____

    _____

# EXERCISE 3.10    MAKING POSITIVE AND NEGATIVE PERCEPTIONS

## Purpose:
1.    To understand how judgments are made from different perspectives.

## Directions:
1.    For each of the following situations, give a positive and a negative perception.

---

1.    You see a "thirty-something" aged man leaning across a table and holding the hands of an older woman in a restaurant.

*Positive:*

*Negative:*

2.    You see a teenager giving money to a well-dressed man in the street.

*Positive:*

*Negative:*

3.    You see the police pull up to your neighbor's house with all lights flashing.

*Positive:*

*Negative:*

4.    You see a large, black dog standing over a screaming child lying on the ground.

*Positive:*

*Negative:*

**Questions:**

1. Which perceptions were easiest to make--positive or negative? Why?

   _____

   _____

   _____

2. What influenced your first reaction to each statement? Why?

   _____

   _____

   _____

   _____

   _____

3. What does this exercise tell you about understanding a situation from the perspective of others?

   _____

   _____

   _____

| | |
|---|---|
| Perception | Interpersonal Perception |
| Selective Perception | Halo Effect |
| Horn Effect | Passive Perception |
| Active Perception | Impression Formation |
| Primacy Effect | Recency Effect |
| Implicit Personality Theory | Personal Constructs |
| Cognitive Complexity | Attributions |

| | |
|---|---|
| The process of selecting, organizing, and interpreting our observations of other people. | The arousal of any of our senses. |
| Attributing a variety of positive qualities to those we like. | Directing our attention to specific stimuli and consequently ignoring others. |
| Perception that occurs because our senses are in operations. | Attributing a variety of negative qualities to those we dislike. |
| The process of forming a general collection of perceptions about another person. | Seeking out specific information through intentional observation and questioning. |
| Placing heavy emphasis on the most recent information we have observed about another to form or modify our impression of another. | Placing heavy emphasis upon the first pieces of information that we observe about another to form an impression. |
| Specific qualities or attributes we associate with each person we know. | Our own set of beliefs and hypotheses about what people are like. |
| The reasons we develop to explain the behaviors of others. | The level of ability to develop a sophisticated set of personal constructs. |

| Correspondent Inference Theory | Causal Attribution Theory |
|---|---|
| Indirect Perception Checking | Direct Perception Checking |

| One theory of attribution that is based upon determining whether a person's actions are caused by circumstance, a stimulus, or the person. | One theory of attribution that is based on determining how intentional a person's actions are. |
|---|---|
| Asking for confirmation or refutation from the observed person of an interpretation of a perception about him or her. | Seeking additional information to confirm or refute interpretations you are making through passive perception. |

# CHAPTER 4
# LISTENING AND RESPONDING

## OBJECTIVES

After studying the material in this chapter of *Interpersonal Communication: Relating to Others* and completing the exercises in this section of the study guide, you should understand:

1. the difference between hearing and listening,
2. how selecting, attending, understanding, and remembering are part of the listening process,
3. the four reasons for listening,
4. how focusing on your own agenda, emotional noise, criticizing the speaker, rate of information, information overload, and external noise all interfere with effective listening behavior,
5. the four levels of learning a skill and how they relate to listening,
6. how to improve your listening skills by stopping, looking, and listening,
7. how to set goals for improving your listening habits,
8. how to use the responding skills to let others know you are listening to understand, and
9. how to become an active listener.

## STUDY QUESTIONS

You should be able to answer the following questions:

1. What is the difference between hearing and listening?
2. What are the four elements of the listening process?
3. What are the reasons we listen?
4. What is empathy?
5. What are the barriers to effective listening?
6. Why do emotional "hot buttons" interfere with listening effectively?
7. How do the levels of learning a skill relate to listening behavior?
8. What are the ways you can improve your listening skills?
9. What are the goal-oriented strategies we can use to improve listening?
10. What are the responding skills we can use to let others know we are listening?
11. What are the steps to responding with empathy?
12. How can you improve your responding skills?

# EXERCISE 4.1    CHOOSING WHAT TO HEAR

## Purposes:
1.    To become aware of the vast amount of stimuli affecting your listening.
2.    To learn to attend to specific stimuli (sounds).

## Directions:
1.    Choose a cassette or CD of your favorite band, orchestra, or artist.
2.    Close your eyes and listen to the recording.
3.    While blocking other sounds out, focus on:
     a.    the percussion instruments (distinguish drums, piano, etc.)
     b.    the stringed instruments (distinguish bass guitar, rhythm guitar, violin)
     c.    the wind instruments (distinguish saxophone, trumpet, trombone)
     d.    the words to the song (if any)
4.    Open your eyes and try to focus on the same sounds listed above.

        Name of cassette or CD                    Sounds identified

## Questions:

1.    Why can't you focus on all the sounds at the same time?

_____

_____

2.    Which sounds are easiest to distinguish?  Why?

_____

_____

3.    Why is it easier to focus on a single sound with your eyes closed?

_____

_____

_____

## EXERCISE 4.2    EXAMINING YOUR TYPES OF LISTENING

**Purposes:**
1.    To investigate how many types of listening you do.
2.    To learn which types of listening you do most often.

**Directions:**
1.    Record with a tape recorder as many listening experiences as you can for a one day period of time.
2.    Evaluate the main purpose of the listening you were doing--listening for enjoyment, to learn, to evaluate, or to empathize.
3.    Describe the listening event and identify the type of listening.

EXPERIENCES                                    TYPE OF LISTENING

1.

2.

3.

4.

5.

6.

7.

8.

9.

10.

11.

12.

**Questions:**
1.    Which type of listening did you do most often?


2.    What can you do to get more variety in your listening opportunities?

## EXERCISE 4.3    LISTENING AND RELATIONSHIPS

**Purposes:**

1.    To define listening
2.    To compare listening ability and level of attraction to the listener.
3.    To identify characteristics of effective and ineffective listeners.

**Directions:**

1.    List the three best listeners you know.  Indicate your relationship to each person.
2.    List the three worst listeners you know.  Indicate your relationship to each person.
3.    List the characteristics of the best and the worst listeners.


| BEST LISTENERS | RELATIONSHIP | CHARACTERISTICS |
| --- | --- | --- |
|  |  |  |
|  |  |  |
|  |  |  |


| WORST LISTENERS | RELATIONSHIP | CHARACTERISTICS |
| --- | --- | --- |
|  |  |  |
|  |  |  |

**Questions:**

1.      How many of the best listeners were people you do not like or are not attracted to? Why are you not attracted to these people?

2.      How many of the worst listeners were people you do like or are attracted to? Why are you attracted to these people?

3.      Which characteristics are similar for the best listeners and the worst listeners?

4.      Which characteristics are different?

## EXERCISE 4.4    SWEARING MORE, LISTENING LESS?

**Purpose:**
1.    To determine how often you "hear" profanity in conversations.

**Directions:**
1.    For the next few days, listen carefully to conversations around you--in public places, in private conversations, on television.
2.    Listen for any offensive language and profane words or phrases.
3.    List all the offensive language that you hear.

| OFFENSIVE LANGUAGE | WHERE YOU HEARD IT |
|---|---|
| | |

**Questions:**

1.    What were you reactions to the language?


2.    How did other people respond to the language?

## EXERCISE 4.5     TRIGGERING YOUR EMOTIONS

**Purposes:**
1.     To identify the words, phrases, topics, and behaviors that create an emotional reaction in you (positive or negatively).
2.     To examine your listening effectiveness when hearing trigger words.

**Directions:**
1.     Make a list of words, phrases, topics, and behaviors to which you have an emotional reaction.
2.     Analyze how these words, phrases, and concepts interfere or enhance your listening effectiveness.

WORDS _____ REACTIONS _____




PHRASES _____ REACTIONS _____




TOPICS _____ REACTIONS _____




BEHAVIORS _____ REACTIONS _____

## Questions:

1. What category are most of your "hot buttons" in--words, phrases, or topics?

2. What makes you have emotional reactions to the items you listed above--values, upbringing, etc.?

3. How can you control your reactions so that they do not interfere to your ability to listen to others effectively?

# EXERCISE 4.6    INTERFERING BARRIERS TO YOUR LISTENING ABILITY

## Purpose:

1.    To become aware of the barriers that prevent your from being an effective listener.

## Directions:

1.    For each of the following listening barriers, list the circumstances during which you have difficulty listening to others effectively.


*Focusing on the person:*    _____

_____


*Emotional noise:*    _____

_____


*Criticizing the speaker:*    _____

_____


*Information rate:*    _____

_____


*Information overload:*    _____

_____


*External noise:*    _____

_____

# EXERCISE 4.7     PAYING ATTENTION TO WHAT?

## Purpose:
To help you become aware of your listening attention span.

## Directions:
1.     Listen to a daily News broadcast on television or radio.
2.     At the beginning of the broadcast, set a timer at a random number of minutes. Or have a roommate ring a bell or whistle at random intervals.
3.     When the bell rings, write what you were thinking. Or write what you were thinking when your roommate signals in some predetermined way to you.
4.     Repeat this same procedure at least five times during a one-half hour news broadcast.


*First signal:* _____


*Second signal:* _____


*Third signal:* _____


*Fourth signal:* _____


*Fifth signal:* _____


## Questions:

1.     How often were you actually paying attention to the broadcast?


2.     How often were you thinking of something related to the topic being discussed on the News?


3.     How often were you thinking of something totally unrelated to the broadcast?

## EXERCISE 4.8    CHALLENGING YOUR LISTENING

**Purpose:**

1.    To practice evaluative listening skills.

**Directions:**

1.    Attend a speech on campus, watch a speaker on CNN, or watch a documentary news show on television.
2.    Write down the main facts from the presentation, analyze the reasoning, and record the evidence used to support the speaker's position.

MAIN FACTS:

_____

_____

_____

TYPE OF REASONING USED:

_____

_____

_____

EXAMPLES OF EVIDENCE GIVEN FOR SUPPORT:

_____

_____

_____

_____

**Questions:**

1.    Did you agree or disagree with the speaker? How were you able to decide if you agreed or disagreed with the speaker?

2.    How difficult was it to concentrate on the speaking event you chose? What interfered with your concentration?

# EXERCISE 4.9     ASSESSING YOUR LISTENING BEHAVIOR

**Purpose:**
1.     To determine your listening behavior.
2.     To help you decide which areas of behavior should be improved to increase your listening abilities.

**Directions:**
1.     Respond to each statement below with a number as follows:

|   |   |   |
|---|---|---|
| 1 | = | Always false |
| 2 | = | Usually false |
| 3 | = | Sometimes false |
| 4 | = | Usually true |
| 5 | = | Always true |

_____ 1.     I have a difficult time separating important and unimportant ideas when I listen to others.

_____ 2.     I check new information against what I already know when I listen to others.

_____ 3.     I have an idea what others will say when I listen to them.

_____ 4.     I am sensitive to others' feelings when I listen to them.

_____ 5.     I think about what I am going to say next when I listen to others.

_____ 6.     I focus on the process of communication that is occurring between me and others when I listen to them.

_____ 7.     I cannot wait for others to finish talking so I can take my turn.

_____ 8.     I try to understand the meanings that are being created when I communicate with others.

_____ 9.     I focus on determining whether others understand what I said when they are talking.

_____ 10.     I ask others to elaborate when I am not sure what they mean.

To find your score, first reverse your responses for the ***odd-numbered*** items (if you wrote 1, make it 5; if you wrote 2, make it 4; if you wore 3, leave it as 3; if you wrote 4, make it 2; if you wrote 5, make it 1). Next, add the numbers next to each statement. Scores range from 10 to 50. The higher your score, the better your listening behavior. (Reproduced for student use from *Interpersonal Communication: Relating to Others.*)

# EXERCISE 4.10     WATCHING AND LISTENING

## Purpose:

1.     To practice maintaining eye contact to let the other person know you are listening and to keep focused on what the other person is saying.

## Directions:

1.     During your conversations for the next few days, make a conscious effort to maintain eye contact with your partner in conversation.

2.     While you are listening and talking, maintain direct eye contact while you mentally count to 5.

3.     Practice this until it becomes a natural ability.  (You will not be able to concentrate fully on the topic of conversation while counting, but you will "get the feel" for maintaining effective eye contact.)

| | |
|---|---|
| Listening | Hearing |
| Selecting | Attending |
| Understanding | Remembering |
| Responding | Empathy |
| Sympathy | Emotional Noise |
| Paraphrasing | |

| | |
|---|---|
| The physiological process of decoding sounds. | The process of selecting, attending, understanding, remembering and responding to sounds and messages. |
| The process of focusing on a particular sound or message. | The process of sorting through various sounds competing for your attention. |
| Recalling information that has been communicated. | Assigning meaning to messages. |
| To feel what others are feeling, rather than just to acknowledge that he or she is feeling a certain way. | Confirming your understanding of a message. |
| Occurs when our emotional arousal interferes with communication effectiveness. | To acknowledge that someone may be feeling bad. |
| | Checking the accuracy of your understanding of a message by offering a verbal summary of your partners message. |

# CHAPTER 5
# COMMUNICATING NONVERBALLY

## OBJECTIVES

After studying the material in this chapter of *Interpersonal Communication: Relating to Others* and completing the exercises in this section of the study guide, you should understand:

1.  the importance of studying nonverbal communication because it focuses on feelings and attitudes, it is more believable than verbal messages, and it impacts our interpersonal relationships,
2.  how nonverbal communication is ambiguous, continuous, multichanneled, and culture based,
3.  the different codes or types of nonverbal communication that is used to communicate messages,
4.  how to interpret immediacy, arousal, and dominance messages, and
5.  how to improve your ability to interpret messages by considering the context of the message, looking for clusters of clues, having longer relationships with others, and checking your perceptions of messages with others.

## STUDY QUESTIONS

You should be able to answer the following questions:

1.  Why is it important to learn about nonverbal communication?
2.  What role does nonverbal communication play in relationship development?
3.  Why is nonverbal communication difficult and challenging to study?
4.  What categories of nonverbal communication are there?
5.  What is kinesics?
6.  What are the four stages of "quasi-courtship behavior?"
7.  What kinesic behaviors contribute to perceptions of liking?
8.  What are the different functions of body movement and gestures?
9.  What are the four functions for eye contact in interpersonal interactions?
10. What are the six primary emotional categories that identify our facial expressions?
11. How is the voice a primary tool for communicating information about relationships?
12. What is proxemics?
13. Describe each of E. T. Hall's spatial zones.
14. What is territoriality and how do we mark our territory?

15. Why is the use of touch important and when are we likely to initiate the use of touch with others?

16. How does personal appearance relate to interpersonal interactions?

17. What are the three primary dimensions that we use to interpret nonverbal cues?

18. What is the function of arousal cues?

19. What do dominance cues communicate to others?

20. How can you improve your ability to interpret nonverbal messages?

## EXERCISE 5.1    FORMING FIRST IMPRESSIONS

**Purpose:**

1.    To become aware of the nonverbal cues that you use in making first impressions.

**Directions:**

1.    Go to a public place--shopping center, library, campus shopping area, etc.
2.    Observe three different people.
3.    Fill out the following survey form.
4.    Optional:  Check out your impressions.

## PERSON #1

AGE

_____

OCCUPATION

_____

POLITICAL
ORIENTATION

_____

MUSIC
PREFERENCE

_____

FAVORITE
PASTIME

_____

RELIGIOUS
AFFILIATION

_____

RELATIONSHIP
TO OTHERS

_____

PERSONALITY
CHARACTERISTICS
(outgoing, athletic, shy,
funny, intelligent, etc.)

_____

## PERSON #2

AGE

_____

OCCUPATION

_____

POLITICAL
ORIENTATION

_____

MUSIC
PREFERENCE

_____

FAVORITE
PASTIME

_____

RELIGIOUS
AFFILIATION

_____

RELATIONSHIP
TO OTHERS

_____

PERSONALITY
CHARACTERISTICS
(outgoing, athletic, shy,
funny, intelligent, etc.)

_____

## PERSON #3

AGE

_____

OCCUPATION

_____

POLITICAL
ORIENTATION

_____

MUSIC
PREFERENCE

_____

FAVORITE
PASTIME

_____

RELIGIOUS
AFFILIATION

_____

RELATIONSHIP
TO OTHERS

_____

PERSONALITY
CHARACTERISTICS
(outgoing, athletic, shy,
funny, intelligent, etc.)

_____

## **Questions**:

1.      What nonverbal cues do you use most often?


        _____


        _____


2.      What was the most difficult judgment for you to make?  Why?


        _____


        _____


3.      What was the easiest judgment for you to make?  Why?


        _____


        _____

# EXERCISE 5.2    CONFUSING NONVERBAL COMMUNICATION

## Purposes:
1.    To understand the ambiguity of nonverbal communication.
2.    To monitor your own nonverbal behavior.

## Directions:
1.    Monitor your communication interactions for the next few days.
2.    Report on two interpersonal interactions where there were communication problems associated with the nonverbal meaning of a message.
3.    Use the following form to report your observations.

### *INTERACTION #1:*

TIME: _____

PLACE: _____

RELATIONSHIP TO THE OTHER PERSON: _____

NONVERBAL CUE THAT CREATED THE PROBLEM: _____

_____

TYPE OF PROBLEM: _____

_____

EFFECTS OR OUTCOME OF PROBLEM: _____

_____

HOW COULD THE PROBLEM HAVE BEEN AVOIDED? _____

_____

_____

### *INTERACTION #2:*

TIME: _____

PLACE: _____

RELATIONSHIP TO THE OTHER PERSON: _____

NONVERBAL CUE THAT CREATED THE PROBLEM: _____

_____

TYPE OF PROBLEM: _____

_____

EFFECTS OR OUTCOME OF PROBLEM: _____

_____

HOW COULD THE PROBLEM HAVE BEEN AVOIDED? _____

_____

_____

**_INTERACTION #3:_**

TIME: _____

PLACE: _____

RELATIONSHIP TO THE OTHER PERSON: _____

NONVERBAL CUE THAT CREATED THE PROBLEM: _____

_____

TYPE OF PROBLEM: _____

_____

EFFECTS OR OUTCOME OF PROBLEM: _____

_____

HOW COULD THE PROBLEM HAVE BEEN AVOIDED? _____

_____

_____

## EXERCISE 5.3    CHALLENGING CONCLUSIONS

**Purpose:**
1.    To investigate the difficulty in making accurate interpretations of nonverbal behavior.
2.    To determine the effect of relationship on the accuracy of your interpretations.

**Directions:**
1.    For the next few days, observe the nonverbal behavior of five friends or family members focusing on a specific incident or situation for each observation.
2.    Record your interpretation of each person's nonverbal behavior.
3.    Share your interpretations with the other people to assess your accuracy in comparison with their explanation.

| RELATIONSHIP OF SUBJECT | SITUATION | INTERPRETATION OF BEHAVIOR | EXPLANATION OF OTHER |
|---|---|---|---|
| | | | |
| | | | |
| | | | |
| | | | |
| | | | |

### Questions:

1.  How did your accuracy of interpretation relate to the level of your relationship with the subjects?

    _____

    _____

    _____

2.  How did your interpretations compare to the explanations of the others?

    _____

    _____

    _____

3.  What behaviors were the most confusing for you?  Why?

    _____

    _____

    _____

4.  What behaviors were the easiest to interpret accurately?  Why?

    _____

    _____

    _____

## EXERCISE 5.4      GROWING UP WITH NONVERBAL RULES

**Purposes:**
1.      To identify the nonverbal rules you learned as a child.
2.      To assess the impact of those rules on your current behavior.

**Directions:**
1.      List the rules you learned to govern your behavior as a child.
2.      State how you learned the rules.
3.      Analyze the impact these rules have on your behavior now.

| RULE | HOW LEARNED | IMPACT ON CURRENT BEHAVIOR |
|---|---|---|
| *Example:*<br>*Remove shoes before coming into the house* | *Parents would stare at our feet if we came in with our shoes on and point to the door* | *I don't take my shoes off when entering my home, but I still take my shoes off when I visit my parents, and I make my children take off their shoes at the grandparents' home.* |
|  |  |  |
|  |  |  |
|  |  |  |

# EXERCISE 5.5    BREAKING THE RULES

## Purpose:
1.    To recognize the importance of nonverbal rules to others.

## Directions:
1.    Identify three nonverbal communication rules that exist in your home, school, and work situations.
2.    Choose one rule from your list and violate the rule.
3.    Write the consequences of the rule breaking exercise. (Remember not to break a rule that would infringe on the right of the other person!)

| SITUATION | RULE | CONSEQUENCES |
|-----------|------|--------------|
| HOME | | |
| SCHOOL | | |
| WORK | | |

CONSEQUENCES OF BREAKING A RULE: _____

_____

_____

_____

# EXERCISE 5.6     PLAYING "I SPY" THE NONVERBAL FUNCTIONS

## Purposes:
1.     To identify the functions of kinesics behavior--emblems, illustrators, affect displays, regulators, and adaptors.
2.     To become aware of your use of each of the functions.

## Directions:
1.     Locate two examples of nonverbal behavior for each of the functional categories above.  A soap opera, television sit-com, or any interpersonal interaction can be used as a source.
2.     Ask a friend or family member to identify examples of the way you use each of the behaviors.

FUNCTION               WHERE I FOUND IT     HOW THE BEHAVIOR  WAS PERFORMED

EMBLEMS

1.

2.


ILLUSTRATORS

1.

2.


AFFECT DISPLAYS

1.

2.


REGULATORS

1.

2.


ADAPTORS

1.

2.

Give the next copy of the "I Spy" form to your friend.  Have your friend or family member record times you use two examples of the nonverbal functions of body movement.

| FUNCTION | WHEN YOU DID IT | HOW YOU PERFORMED THE BEHAVIOR |
|---|---|---|

EMBLEMS

1.

2.


ILLUSTRATORS

1.

2.


AFFECT DISPLAYS

1.

2.


REGULATORS

1.

2.


ADAPTORS

1.

2.

**EXERCISE 5.7     COMPUTING NONVERBAL MESSAGES**

<u>**Purposes**</u>:
1.      To learn how to use emoticons when sending computer generated messages..
2.      To add emotional impact to computer messages.

<u>**Directions**</u>:
1.      Write a message to someone through the campus E-mail system or send a
        computer written letter to a friend, using the emoticons identified in the *HomePC*
        article summarized in *Interpersonal Communication: Relating to Others* to add
        emotional impact.

## EXERCISE 5.8     MONITORING YOUR NONVERBAL BEHAVIOR

**Purpose**:
1.      To recognize how your own nonverbal behavior expresses your emotions.

**Directions**:
1.      Over the next few days, pay attention to the different emotions you are feeling.
2.      Monitor the nonverbal expressions of each emotion and record the results in the form below.

| SITUATION | EMOTION I WAS FEELING | NONVERBAL EXPRESSION USED |
|-----------|----------------------|---------------------------|
| 1. | | |
| 2. | | |
| 3. | | |
| 4. | | |
| 5. | | |
| 6. | | |
| 7. | | |
| 8. | | |

## EXERCISE 5.9    INTERPRETING THE PRIMARY DIMENSIONS OF NONVERBAL CUES

**Purpose:**

1.    To learn to recognize examples of immediacy (liking), arousal (responding), and dominance (power).

**Directions:**

1.    Observe pairs of people interacting at work, at home, or at school.  Six different couples may be used or three may be used if all of the dimensions are demonstrated.
2.    Record nonverbal behaviors that indicate both high and low levels of immediacy between two of the individuals in two different couples.
3.    Record nonverbal behaviors that indicate both high and low levels of arousal between the individuals in two different couples.
4.    Record nonverbal behaviors that indicate both high and low levels of power between the individuals in two different couples.

| LOW LEVEL CUES OF BEHAVIOR | HIGH LEVEL CUES OF BEHAVIOR |
|---|---|

**IMMEDIACY**

Posture _____        Posture _____

Body orientation _____        Body orientation _____

Eye contact _____        Eye contact _____

Gestures _____        Gestures _____

Movement _____        Movement _____

Touch _____        Touch _____

Space _____        Space _____

Voice _____        Voice _____

Facial Expression _____        Facial Expression _____

**AROUSAL**

Posture _____            Posture _____

Body orientation _____            Body orientation _____

Eye contact _____            Eye contact _____

Gestures _____            Gestures _____

Movement _____            Movement _____

Touch _____            Touch _____

Space _____            Space _____

Voice _____            Voice _____

Facial Expression _____            Facial Expression _____

**DOMINANCE**

Posture _____            Posture _____

Body orientation _____            Body orientation _____

Eye contact _____            Eye contact _____

Gestures _____            Gestures _____

Movement _____            Movement _____

Touch _____            Touch _____

Space _____            Space _____

Voice _____            Voice _____

Facial Expression _____            Facial Expression _____

**EXERCISE 5.10     MANAGING YOUR PERSONAL NEEDS NONVERBALLY**

**Purpose:**

1.     To become aware of the nonverbal cues you use to manage your personal needs or to adapt to uncomfortable situations.

**Directions:**

1.     Monitor your behavior over the next two days.
2.     Identify the situation and the feeling you are having, especially feeling uncomfortable, anxious, or stressed
3.     List the nonverbal behaviors you use to cope with these feelings.

SITUATIONS                          NONVERBAL BEHAVIORS

1.


2.


3.


4.


5.


6.

7.

8.

9.

10.

**EXERCISE 5.11    DISTRACTING EACH OTHER**

**Purpose:**
1.    To become aware of your distracting nonverbal mannerisms or behaviors.
2.    To help a partner identify his/her distracting nonverbal mannerisms or behaviors.

**Directions:**
1.    List any behaviors that your partner performs that are distracting or annoying to you.
2.    Have your partner list any behaviors that you perform that are distracting or annoying to him/her.
3.    To help you and your partner understand the circumstances in which you each perform the behaviors
.
You fill out this form about your partner.

**BEHAVIORS THAT ANNOY/DISTRACT ME**                **SITUATION**

1.


_____


2.


_____


3.


_____


4.


_____


5.


_____

**BEHAVIORS THAT ANNOY/DISTRACT OTHERS**     <u>**SITUATION**</u>

1.

_____

2.

_____

3.

_____

4.

_____

5.

_____

<u>**Questions**</u>**:**

1.      What behaviors were you unaware of doing?

_____

_____

2.      What changes would you like to make in your nonverbal behavior?

_____

_____

3.      How do you think you can change your nonverbal behaviors?

_____

## EXERCISE 5.12     GAZING AND TALKING

**Purposes:**
1.    To learn to maintain eye contact longer during interpersonal conversations.
2.    To compare your use of eye contact between people whom you like and people whom you dislike.

**Directions:**
1.    Carry on a two minute conversation with two people whom you like and two people for whom you don't have positive feelings.
2.    During each conversation, try to maintain direct eye contact for the count of five (five seconds).
3.    Rate the level of difficulty of maintaining eye contact with each person, according to a 1-5 scale with 1 being very easy and 5 being very difficult.

|     | NAME OF PARTNER | LEVEL OF LIKING | RATING |
| --- | --- | --- | --- |
| 1.  |     |     |     |
| 2.  |     |     |     |
| 3.  |     |     |     |
| 4.  |     |     |     |

**Questions:**

1.    Was it easier to maintain eye contact with the people you like than the people you do not like as well?  Why?

_____

_____

2.    What does this exercise tell you about eye contact and interpersonal communication?

_____

_____

# EXERCISE 5.13    SINGING ABOUT EYES

## Purpose:
1.    To become more aware of the importance of eyes to interpersonal relationships.

## Directions:
1.    The subject of eyes can be emphasized by listening to music.  Listen to the radio, MTV or VHS stations, or browse through a Record store.
2.    Listen and look for titles of songs that include the word "eyes" and listen for reference to eyes within the verses of the songs.
3.    Record the names of the songs and the artist who recorded the song.  Examples are *I Can See Forever in Your Eyes* by Reba McEntire, *Angel Eyes* by Jeff Healey, *In Your Eyes* by Peter Gabriel, *Eye of the Beholder* by Metallica, *Eyes That See In The Dark* by Kenny Rogers, *Eyes Of The World* by The Grateful Dead.

**TITLE OF THE SONG**                    **ARTIST**

1.

2.

3.

4.

5.

6.

7.

8.

9.

10.

## EXERCISE 5.14    JUDGING BY VOICE

### Purpose:
1.     To determine how vocal characteristics affect your perceptions of others.

### Directions:
1.     Turn on a television show that you have never watched before and tape the show.
2.     Go to another room where you cannot see the television, but you can hear the voices.
3.     Listen to the voices of two actors or speakers.
4.     Write a description of each person, including information such as gender, age, race, educational background, occupation, status, and emotional state.
5.     Rewind and play the tape of the show to determine how accurate your description is.

## DESCRIPTION

ACTOR #1

_____

ACTOR #2

_____

### Questions:

1.     How accurate were you with your description?


2.     Which are the most useful features of paralanguage in determining the above information?


3.     What cautions should you take in making judgments about others based only on vocal cues?


4.     In what real life situations does voice affect perception?


5.     How might voice affect interpersonal communication interactions?

# EXERCISE 5.15    EMPHASIZING WITH VOCAL NONVERBAL CUES

## Purpose:
1.    To become aware of the meaning changes that can take place by emphasis on a single word in a sentence.

## Directions:
1.    Repeat the following sentences, putting emphasis on a different word each time.
2.    Listen for the difference in meaning as you change the emphasis on the different words.

      A.    Where did you get that?
              **WHERE** did you get that?
              Where **DID** you get that?
              Where did **YOU** get that?
              Where did you **GET** that?
              Where did you get **THAT**?

      B.    He did not steal her purse.

      C.    Why did you drive there?

      D.    Are you going to that party with them?

      E.    I really hate this.

## Questions:

1.    How do the changes in vocal emphasis affect the relationship aspect of each message?

2.    What different emotions are illustrated through the vocal emphasis changes of each of the message?

**EXERCISE 5.16    COMMUNICATING ABOUT YOU IN YOUR PLACE**

**Purposes:**
1.    To understand how you announce ownership of your space by marking it.
2.    To investigate what your "place" communicates about you.

**Directions:**
1.    Identify a place that you consider to be yours--bedroom, kitchen, den, residence hall room, office.
2.    Observe this space you consider to be yours.  How is it decorated?  What things do you have sitting around?  How is it arranged?  How do you let others know it is "your" space--what markers do you use?
3.    Write a description of your place based on your observations.

*Example:*
        *I consider the kitchen in our house to be my place.  The kitchen is large and very open.  In the center there is an island with the stove top on one side and a table level bar on the other side with chairs.  The furniture is country style--antique chairs, dry sink, and Hoosier cabinet.  The walls are white and the cabinets and woodworking in light oak. The table and other cabinets in the eating area are light oak and country in style.  The walls are decorated with country paintings and cross-stitch articles.  The refrigerator door is covered with pictures of family members.  The countertops are usually neat and clean, with a few decorative pottery pieces and baskets.  There is a little sign on the entrance wall that says:  "Welcome to _____'s kitchen."*

**Your description of "your" place:**

**Questions:**
1.    What does your place (territory) communicate about you?

2.    How does the arrangement of your place affect my communication with others?

3.    What could you change about my place that would change the communication interactions?

| | |
|---|---|
| Nonverbal Communication | Kinesics |
| Emblems | Illustrators |
| Affect Display | Regulators |
| Adaptors | Intimate Space |
| Personal Space | Social Space |
| Public Space | Territoriality |
| Immediacy | Arousal |

| | |
|---|---|
| The study of human movement and gestures. | Behavior other than written or spoken language that creates meaning for someone. |
| Nonverbal behavior that accompanies a verbal message and either contradicts, accents, or complements it. | Nonverbal cues that have specific, generally understood meaning in a given culture and may substitute for a word or phrase. |
| Nonverbal messages that help to control the interaction or level of communication between people. | Nonverbal behavior that communicates emotions. |
| Zone of personal space most often used for very personal or intimate conversation, ranging from 0 to 18 inches. | Nonverbal behaviors that help satisfy a personal need and help a person adapt or respond to the immediate situation. |
| Zone of personal space most often used fro group discussion, ranging from 4 to 12 feet. | Zone of personal space most often used for conversation, ranging from 1 1/2 to 4 feet. |
| The study of how animals and humans use space and objects to communicate occupancy or ownership of space. | Zone of personal space most often used by public speakers or one speaking to many people, ranging beyond 12 feet. |
| The feelings of interest and excitement communicated by such nonverbal cues as vocal expression, facial expression and gestures. | The feelings of liking, pleasure, and closeness communicated by such nonverbal cues as eye contact, forward lean, touch, and open body orientation. |

| Dominance | Perception Check |
|-----------|------------------|

| The skill of asking someone whether your interpretation of his or her nonverbal behavior is accurate. | The feeling of power, status, and control communicated by such nonverbal cues as a relaxed posture, greater personal space, and protected personal space. |
| --- | --- |

# CHAPTER 6
# COMMUNICATING VERBALLY

## OBJECTIVES

After studying the material in this chapter of *Interpersonal Communication: Relating to Others* and completing the exercises in this section of the study guide, you should understand:

1. the relationship between words and their meanings,
2. how words influence us and our culture,
3. how to identify word barriers and know how to manage the barriers,
4. how the words we use affect our relationships with others,
5. the supportive approaches we can use when relating to others, and
6. how to confirm other people's sense of themselves.

## STUDY QUESTIONS

You should be able to answer the following questions:

1. What are symbols, referents, and thoughts?
2. What does it mean when we say "words are arbitrary?"
3. How does communication differ between a high-context and a low-context culture?
4. How does culture impact the meaning of a symbol?
5. Explain how the theory of symbolic interactionism relates to interpersonal communication.
6. Define denotative and connotative as they relate to words.
7. What does it mean when we say that words are abstract or concrete?
8. How do words have power to create, affect thoughts and actions, and affect and reflect culture.
9. Why are the following concepts considered barriers to understanding: bypassing, bafflegab, lack of precision, allness or indexing, static evaluation, polarization, fact-inference, and biased language?
10. How can words help to establish supportive relationships?
11. What are the confirming responses we can use to make others feel good about themselves?
12. What are the seven disconfirming responses we can use to undermine another person's self-worth?

**EXERCISE 6.1    CREATING NEW WORDS**

**Purpose:**
1.    To understand that language is a set of symbols used to create meaning.
2.    To create and change language with your subcultural group.

**Directions:**
1.    Create three new words for objects, events, people, or everyday activities.
2.    Tell at least three friends or family members about these words and what meaning you have given them.
3.    Make up a sentence for each word.
4.    Begin using these words in your conversations with these people and other people.
5.    Record the reactions to the use of these words--asked for an explanation, pretended to understand, tried to use the "new" word, etc.

| WORD | MEANING | SENTENCE | REACTION |
|------|---------|----------|----------|
| *Spood* | *Wanting space* | *Please leave. I'm really spood.* | *My friends caught on and liked the word.* |

## Questions:

1. Were your words nouns, verbs, adjectives, or adverbs?

2. How easy was it to create a new word?

3. Do you think your sub-culture (family and friends) will continue to use your words? Why or why not?

4. Why do we feel the need to create new words?

5. What do the words we create tell us about our culture or sub-culture?

# EXERCISE 6.2    BRIDGING THE GAPS

## Purpose:
1.     To realize that words have different meanings to different people.
2.     To understand how cultural background and age affect word meaning.
3.     To recognize the denotative definition from the connotative definition of words.

## Directions:
1.     Give the denotative meaning and one connotative meaning to each of the words listed below.
2.     Ask two of your friends or family members to also give their meanings to the words. Try to get definitions from people of a different cultural background and age than yours.

| Denotative Definition | Connotative Definition |
|---|---|
| 1.  Chick | 1. |
|  | 2. |
|  | 3. |
| 2.  Grass | 1. |
|  | 2. |
|  | 3. |
| 3.  Square | 1. |
|  | 2. |
|  | 3. |
| 4.  Pot | 1. |
|  | 2. |
|  | 3. |
| 5.  Pig | 1. |
|  | 2. |
|  | 3. |

6. Rap               1.

                        2.

                        3.

**Questions:**

1.      How did your definitions compare to the other two people?

         _____

         _____

         _____

2.      What cultural differences occurred?

         _____

         _____

         _____

3.      How would the difference in the definitions affect understanding between two people?

         _____

         _____

         _____

# EXERCISE 6.3  SPEAKING AMBIGUOUSLY

## Purpose:
1.  To understand the problems of ambiguous language in creating clear messages.

## Directions:
1.  Read the statements printed below.
2.  Answer the question following each statement.
3.  Have three other people answer the questions.
4.  Compare your answers.

| STATEMENT | RESPONSES |
|---|---|
| 1.  James is <u>independently wealthy</u>. What is his total personal worth? | ____  ____  ____  ____ |
| 2.  Mary is <u>quite old</u>. How old is Mary? | ____  ____  ____  ____ |
| 3.  Jim is a <u>heavy smoker</u>. How many cigarettes does he smoke each day? | ____  ____  ____  ____ |
| 4.  Carol watches <u>a lot</u> of television. How many hours a day does she spend watching TV? | ____  ____  ____  ____ |
| 5.  David has been playing the guitar for <u>a long time</u>.  How long had he been playing? | ____  ____  ____  ____ |
| 6.  George, the plumber, is <u>well paid</u> for his service.  What is his hourly wage. | ____  ____  ____  ____ |
| 7.  Today is a <u>very hot</u> day.  What is the temperature? | ____  ____  ____  ____ |
| 8.  Professor Jones let us out of class <u>quite early</u> today.  How many minutes prior to the normal dismissal time did the class finish? | ____  ____  ____  ____ |

## Questions:
1.  What contributed to the differences in interpreting the meaning for the statements?
2.  How could you restate each statement, using more concrete language?

# EXERCISE 6.4    CLEARING UP MY LANGUAGE

## Purpose:
1.    To examine your unclear language patterns in everyday communication events.
2.    To learn others' perceptions of your unclear language patterns.

## Directions:
1.    For the next few days, keep a record of any jargon, words that might offend others, mispronounced or misused words, and repetitive and distracting words.
2.    Without sharing your own perceptions about yourself, ask a close friend or family member share his or her perceptions of your language habits with you.

## JARGON OR TECHNICAL TERMS
(Common terms, word phrases, and acronyms used in your job, our discipline at school, volunteer organizations in which you participate that other people might not understand)

My observation                          Perception from friend or family member

1.

2.

3.

4.

5.


## EMOTIONAL OR OFFENSIVE WORDS
(Words or phrases that might be biased or insensitive to others--language that reflects gender, racial or ethnic biases)

My observation                          Perception from friend or family member

1.

2.

3.

4.

5.

## MISPRONOUNCED OR MISUSED WORDS

(Words or phrases used inappropriately or in imprecise ways, creating lack of clarity)

My observation                    Perception from friend or family member

1.

2.

3.

4.

5.


## ALLNESS WORDS OR PHRASES

(Words or phrases that categorize things, actions, or people into a general group.)

My observation                    Perception from friend or family member

1.

2.

3.

4.

5.

## **Questions:**

1.      In which categories did you find the most examples?


2.      Did your observations of yourself agree with that of your friend or family member?


3.      How can you avoid these words or phrases?

# EXERCISE 6.5    ESTABLISHING SUPPORTIVE RELATIONSHIPS

## Purpose:

1.    To help you understand the ways in which you create either a defensive or supportive atmosphere in an important relationship.

## Directions:

1.    Choose a person with whom you have an important relationship--co-worker, family member, friend, roommate, etc.
2.    Be a teacher and explain the supportive and defensive-arousing communication behaviors as explained in your text.
3.    After you discuss the behaviors with your partner, ask him or her to identify which of the behaviors you use with him or her. Get examples to clarify this explanation, identifying when you use the behavior--a particular subject, a certain mood you are in, a reaction to the way your partner acts, a certain time.
4.    Categorize your behaviors as supportive (confirming) or defense-arousing (disconfirming).
5.    Describe each behavior and the situation in which it occurs.
6.    When you complete the exercise, ask your partner to check the accuracy of the information you recorded.
7.    Fill out the forms on the following pages.

| SUPPORTIVE (CONFIRMING) BEHAVIORS PARTNER REPORTS I USE | SITUATIONS IN WHICH I USE EACH BEHAVIOR |
|---|---|
| 1. | 1. |
| 2. | 2. |
| 3. | 3. |
| 4. | 4. |
| 5. | 5. |

| DEFENSE-AROUSING (DISCONFIRMING) BEHAVIORS I USE | SITUATIONS IN WHICH I USE EACH BEHAVIOR |
|---|---|
| 1. | 1. |
| 2. | 2. |
| 3. | 3. |
| 4. | 4. |
| 5. | 5. |

**Questions:**

1.      In which situations do you use confirming communication behaviors?

2.      In which situations do you use more defense-arousing communication behaviors?

3.      Which supportive communication behaviors do you use most frequently?

4.      Which defense-arousing communication behaviors do you use most frequently?

5.      How could you behave in a more confirming way with your partner and with other people?

(adapted from: Wiemann, M.O. & Adler, R.B. *Looking Out, Looking In* Activities Manual, Holt, Rinehart & Winston)

# EXERCISE 6.6    TALKING IN CODES

## Purpose:
1.    To help you understand how your language is unique to your relationships.

## Directions:
1.    Think of your relationships as subcultures.
2.    Choose a close partner (romantic partner, family member, best friend) and a group to which you belong.
3.    List the words, phrases, or other special language codes you use within each relationship.

PARTNER                                              GROUP

## Questions:

1.    How did you and your partner develop your unique language codes?

2.    How did you learn the special codes of the group to which you belong?

3.    Why don't you use the same language codes in other relationships?

**EXERCISE 6.7     DESCRIBING WHAT YOU MEAN**

**Purpose:**
1.     To practice turning static evaluation statements into descriptive statements.

**Directions:**
1.     Read the statements below.
2.     Rewrite each statement to describe the possible behavior(s) or characteristics that led to the original comment which labeled the person, object, or event without considering change.

---

1.     "That teacher is a bore!"

 

 

2.     "That guy's real macho."

 

 

3.     "Mike's a hard worker."

 

 

4.     "LaKita is a flake!"

 

 

5.     "That car is awesome!"

 

 

## EXERCISE 6.8    EXAMINING REGIONALISMS

**Purpose:**

1.    To help you become aware of words that have different meanings.

**Directions:**

1.    Read all of the words referring to a given item.
2.    Circle the word that you ordinarily use.
3.    If you use more than one word in a group, mark the word you use most frequently.
4.    Ask other people to share the word they use for each item described.  Choose people from different geographical locations and ages.

---

1.    YARD ADJOINING A BARN:

(A) barn lot  (B) barn yard  (C) cow lot  (D) feed lot  (E) farm lot

2.    HEAVY IRON UTENSIL FOR FRYING:

(A) frying pan  (B) skillet  (C) fry pan  (D) creeper  (E) spider

3.    BONE FROM A CHICKEN BREAST:

(A) lucky bone  (B) pully bone  (C) wishbone  (D) breakbone
(E) pullingbone

4.    A TIME OF DAY:

(A) quarter of eleven  (B) quarter to eleven  (C) quarter till  (D) 10:45

5.    PAPER CONTAINER FOR GROCERIES:

(A) bag  (B) toot  (C) grocery sack  (D) grocery bag  (E) sack
(F) poke

6.    CORN EATEN ON COB:

(A) corn-on-the-cob  (B) green corn  (C) sweet corn  (D) roasting ears
(E) sugar corn  (F) garden corn

7.　WORM USED FOR BAIT IN FISHING:

(A) angleworm  (B) fish worm  (C) fishing worm  (D) redworm
(E) earthworm  (F) fishbait  (G) night crawlers


8.　FAMILY WORD FOR FATHER:

(A) dad  (B) daddy  (C) father  (D) pa  (E) papa  (F) pappy  (G) paw
(H) pop


9.　FAMILY WORD FOR MOTHER:

(A) ma  (B) mama  (C) maw  (D) mom  (E) mum  (F) mommy
(G) mother  (H) mammy


10.　SUMMER WORK:

(A) cut the grass  (B) cut the yard  (C) cut the lawn  (D) mow the grass
(E) mow the yard  (F) mow the lawn

| | |
|---|---|
| Symbol | Referent |
| Thought | High-Context Culture |
| Low-Context Culture | Symbolic Interaction |
| Denotative Meaning | Connotative Meaning |
| Linguistic Determinism | World View |
| Bypassing | Malapropism |
| Restricted Code | Jargon |

| | |
|---|---|
| The thing that a symbol represents. | A word, sound, or visual device that represents a thought, concept or object. |
| A culture in which the meaning of messages is highly dependent upon context and nonverbal cues. | The mental process of creating a category, idea, or image triggered by a referent or symbol. |
| A theory that suggests societies are bound together through common use of symbols. | A culture that relies primarily on language to communicate messages. |
| The personal and subjective meaning of a word. | The restrictive or literal meaning of a word. |
| A culturally acquired perspective for interpreting experiences. | A theory that describes how use of language determines or influences thoughts and perceptions. |
| The confusion of one word or phrase for another that sounds similar to it. | Occurs when the same words mean different things to different people. |
| Specialized terms or abbreviations whose meaning is known only to members of a specific group. | Using few words to communicate an idea or concept. |

| | |
|---|---|
| Allness | Indexing |
| Static Evaluation | Polarization |
| Elaborated Code | Confirming Statements |
| Disconfirming Statements | |

| | |
|---|---|
| A way of avoiding allness statements by separating one situation, person, or example from another. | The tendency to use language to make unqualified, often untrue generalizations. |
| Describing and evaluating what we observe in terms of extremes such as good or bad, old or new, beautiful or ugly. | Pronouncing judgment on something without taking changes into consideration. |
| Statements which cause another person to value himself or herself more. | Using many words to communicate an idea or concept. |
| | Statements which cause another person to value himself or herself less. |

# CHAPTER 7
## DIMENSIONS AND PRINCIPLES OF INTERPERSONAL RELATIONSHIPS

## OBJECTIVES

After studying this chapter in the text, *Interpersonal Communication: Relating to Others*, and completing the exercises in this section of the study guide, you should understand:

1. the difference between a relationship of circumstance and a relationship of choice,
2. the role that the dimensions of trust, intimacy, and power play in interpersonal relationships,
3. how communication qualities change as relationships move through the stages of development and decay,
4. how interpersonal communication is affected by the stage of the relationship, and
5. how relationships work by learning the eight principles of interpersonal relationships.

## STUDY QUESTIONS

You should be able to answer the following questions:

1. What is the definition of interpersonal relationship?
2. How are relationships of circumstance and relationships of choice different?
3. What are the five different types of trust?
4. What is intimacy and how do we communicate varying levels to others?
5. What are the three types of power in relationships and how is power communicated?
6. How does the quality of communication in relationships change as a relationship grows and decays?
7. What are the 10 stages of relationship development and how does the communication change from one stage to another?
8. How are interpersonal relationships processes, systems, mutually defined, renegotiated, related to roles, perceived differently, defined by past relationships, and a balance between comfort and intimacy?

## EXERCISE 7.1    TRUSTING OTHERS

**Purpose:**
1.    To examine the amount of trust you have for others.

**Directions:**
1.    List 10 people with whom you interact in on a regular basis.
2.    For each person, write down the type of trust that characterizes your relationship: in ability, in regard for your welfare, in protecting privileged information, or in commitment to the relationship.
3.    Rate the amount of trust you have in each person, using the following scale:

Very little trust    = 1 --------------> very much trust = 10

| PERSON | TYPE OF TRUST | AMOUNT OF TRUST |
|--------|--------------|-----------------|
| 1. | | |
| 2. | | |
| 3. | | |
| 4. | | |
| 5. | | |
| 6. | | |
| 7. | | |
| 8. | | |
| 9. | | |
| 10. | | |

## Questions:

1. Are your rankings consistently high or consistently low? Why do you think that happened?

2. How would you define the relationship (acquaintance, close friend, family member, etc.) you have with the people in whom you indicated a high level of trust? A low level of trust?

3. How can you explain the reason for each of your rankings?

4. What general observations can you make about how trusting you are of others?

## EXERCISE 7.2    WATCHING FOR POWER CUES

**Purpose:**
1.    To learn to recognize cues that indicate power during communication interactions.

**Directions:**
1.    Observe three different pairs of friends and/or family members engaged in a debate or an argument.
2.    List all of the powerful and powerless communication cues used by each person

|  | POWERFUL CUES | POWERLESS CUES |
|---|---|---|
| COUPLE #1 | | |
| COUPLE #2 | | |
| COUPLE #3 | | |

**Questions:**
1.    Which "powerful" cues did people use most often?
2.    Which "powerless" cues did people use most often?
3.    To what degree were each of the interactants affected by their partner's use of powerful cues?
4.    To what extent were each of the interactants affected by their partner's use of powerless cues?

# EXERCISE 7.3     COMPARING QUALITIES OF COMMUNICATION

## Purpose:
1.    To become aware of how your qualities of communication change with different types of relationships.

## Directions:
1.    Choose three different relationships you have: a family member (FM), a close friend (CF), and a new friend (NF).
2.    Think about your communication interactions with each person.
3.    On the continua below, place each relationship in the appropriate position to indicate how much of each quality was present in your interaction with each person.  For example, your first continuum might look like this:

NARROW<---------NF-------------------------FM------CF--->BROAD

---

NARROW<----------------------------------------------------------------->BROAD

STYLIZED<--------------------------------------------------------------->UNIQUE

DIFFICULT<------------------------------------------------------------->EFFICIENT

RIGID<------------------------------------------------------------------->FLEXIBLE

AWKWARD<------------------------------------------------------------->SMOOTH

PUBLIC<--------------------------------------------------------------->PERSONAL

HESITANT<----------------------------------------------------------->SPONTANEOUS

OVERT JUDGMENT                                          OVERT JUDGMENT
SUSPENDED<----------------------------------------------------------->GIVEN

## Questions:

1.    What differences do you see among the relationships?


2.    How do you explain the differences?

# EXERCISE 7.4    JUDGING COMMUNICATION QUALITIES AND GENDER

## Purpose:
1. To examine the differences in communication qualities in a variety of relationships.
2. To determine the degree of personalization, synchronization, and difficulty you use in family member, close friend, and new friend interactions.
3. To determine the degree of personalization, synchronization, and difficulty you use with same-sex friends and with opposite sex friends.

## Directions:
1. Choose a person from each of the following categories: same-sex family member (SFM), opposite sex family member (OFM), same-sex close friend (SCF), opposite sex close friend (OCF), same-sex new friend (SNF), and opposite sex new friend (OSF).
2. Think of a communication interaction with each of the chosen people.
3. On the continua below, place each relationship in the appropriate position to indicate how much of each quality was present in your interaction with each one.

---

## FAMILY MEMBERS:
### Personalization

High--------------------------------------------------------------------------Low

### Synchronization

High--------------------------------------------------------------------------Low

### Difficulty

High--------------------------------------------------------------------------Low

## CLOSE FRIENDS:

### Personalization

High--------------------------------------------------------------------------Low

### Synchronization

High--------------------------------------------------------------------------Low

### Difficulty

High--------------------------------------------------------------------------Low

**NEW FRIENDS:**

### Personalization

High------------------------------------------------------------------------Low

### Synchronization

High------------------------------------------------------------------------Low

### Difficulty

High------------------------------------------------------------------------Low

## Questions:

1. What differences do you see in the quality of your communication among the relationships?

   _____

   _____

   _____

2. What differences do you see in the quality of your communication among the genders?

   _____

   _____

   _____

3. How do you explain these differences?

   _____

   _____

   _____

# EXERCISE 7.5     CHARTING RELATIONAL DEVELOPMENT

## Purpose:
1. To determine the movement of relationships through stages.
2. To understand how perceptual differences affect relational development.

## Directions:
1. Think of an interpersonal relationship that you have had for at least a year.
2. Plot the development of that relationship from stage to stage over time.
3. Have your relational partner fill out a chart also.
4. Compare your perceptions of how the relationship has developed with your partner's perceptions.

Your chart:

| |
|---|
| Intimacy |
| Intensification |
| Exploration |
| Initiation |
| Pre-Interaction Awareness |

Months -------->

Your partner's chart:

Intimacy

Intensification

Exploration

Initiation

Pre-Interaction Awareness

Months -------->

**Questions**:

1.    What differences are there between your perceptions and your partner's perceptions?

2.    Why do you think you and your partner may see your relationship in different stages of development at a particular time?

3.    What can you tell from the charts about the nature of your relationship?

4.    If you backed up to a previous stage at any point during your relationship try to explain why that happened.

## EXERCISE 7.6     CHANGING RELATIONSHIPS

**Purpose:**
1.     To understand how changes in you and your partners create change in your relationship.
2.     To understand how outside influences create change in your relationships.

**Directions:**
1.     Choose three relationships you have.
2.     Think of ways you and your partners have changed during the time you have known each other.
3.     Think of the events, situations, moods, etc. that have made an impact on your relationship. (One of you may have had an illness, taken a new job, had a death in the family, etc.).

| Define Relationship | Describe changes | Describe impact on relationship |
|---|---|---|
| Husband | I went back to college | I didn't have as much time to spend with him any more, so we began to drift further apart than we had been before I went to school. |
| | | |
| | | |
| | | |

# EXERCISE 7.7    PERCEIVING RELATIONSHIPS

## Purpose:
1.    To understand how perceptions within a relationship differ.

## Directions:
1.    Find a friend who is willing to do this exercise with you.
2.    Each of you are to complete the following:
      a.    describe your perception of the relationship you have with each other.
      b.    describe what you think your partner's perception of the relationship is.
      c.    describe what you think your friend will say is your perception of the relationship.
3.    Compare your responses.

## Questions to answer after completing the exercise:

1.    How similar are your responses about your individual perceptions of the relationship?

_____

_____

2.    What makes your responses different?

_____

_____

3.    How closely were each of you able to predict the other's perception of the relationship (Compare your response to section 1 to your partner's response to section 2)?

_____

_____

4.    What does this exercise tell you about your relationship if all three responses are similar?  Different?

_____

_____

_____

Fill out this form yourself:

| Your perception of the relationship |
| :--- |
| What you think your friend's perception of the relationship is |
| What you think your friend will say your perception of the relationship is |

Give this form to your friend:

| Your perception of the relationship |
| :--- |
| What you think your friend's perception of the relationship is |
| What you think your friend will say your perception of the relationship is |

| | |
|---|---|
| Interpersonal Relationships | Relationships of Circumstance |
| Relationships of Choice | Trust |
| Trustworthy | Intimacy |
| Power | Personalization |
| Synchronization | Communication Difficulty |
| Turning Point | Relational Escalation |
| Relational De-Escalation | |

| | |
|---|---|
| Interpersonal relationships that exist because of the circumstances in which we are born, circumstances in which we work or study, etc. | Those connections we make with other people through interpersonal communication. |
| A quality of a relationship represented by the degree to which the partners believe it is safe to disclose personal information. | Interpersonal relationships we choose to initiate, maintain, and terminate. |
| A quality of a relationship represented by the degree to which a person's sense of self is accepted and confirmed by another person. | A quality we use to describe an individual who can be trusted to accept personal information without exploiting it, support vulnerabilities, and remain in a relationship |
| The degree to which interpersonal communication is personal and unique to the relationship. | A quality of a relationship represented by the degree to which one person can influence another in the direction he or she desires. |
| The level of tension and problems manifested in an interaction. | The degree to which two individuals coordinate the management of their interaction. |
| The upward movement of a relationship toward intimacy through five stages: pre-interaction awareness, initiation, exploration, intensification, and intimacy. | Specific events or interactions which are associated with positive or negative changes in a relationship |
| | The downward movement of a relationship away from intimacy through five stages: turmoil/stagnation, de-intensification, individualizing, separation, and post-interaction. |

# CHAPTER 8
# INITIATING AND ESTABLISHING RELATIONSHIPS

## OBJECTIVES

After studying the material in this chapter of *Interpersonal Communication: Relating to Others* and completing the exercises in this section of the study guide, you should understand:

1. how interpersonal attraction relates to formation and long-term maintenance of relationships,
2. how the elements of physical attraction, credibility, competence and charisma, proximity, similarity, complementarity of needs, relationship potential, and reciprocation of liking affect relationship development,
3. the relationship between attraction, affinity seeking behaviors, and uncertainty reduction strategies,
4. how self-disclosure leads to relationship development,
5. the difference between the social penetration model and the Johari Window model of self-disclosure, and
6. how the eight rules for initiating conversation leads to relationship development.

## STUDY QUESTIONS

You should be able to answer the following questions:

1. What is interpersonal attraction?
2. Explain the difference between short-term initial attraction and long-term maintenance attraction.
3. Describe each of the elements of interpersonal attraction.
4. How is attraction and liking communicated to others?
5. What are the uncertainty reduction strategies?
6. What is self-disclosure in interpersonal relationships?
7. How does self-disclosure move relationships toward intimacy?
8. Why is self-disclosure expected to be reciprocated?
9. Why is self-disclosure risky and based on costs and rewards?
10. What is the social penetration model and how does it relate to relationship development?
11. What are the quadrants of the Johari Window and how do they relate to relationships?
12. Name the eight rules for initiating communication in a new relationship.

## EXERCISE 8.1     OBSERVING OTHERS

### Purpose:
1.     To become aware of the characteristics you consider attractive and repulsive.
2.     To determine the characteristics of others that would lead you to pursue relationships.

### Directions:
1.     At the next social event you attend, observe five different people who you do not know (choose people of different races, cultures, ages, or occupations).
2.     Make a list of the qualities each person has that are attractive to you.
3.     Make a list of the qualities each person has that are unattractive to you.
4.     Indicate which of the people you would like to get to know better, if you had the chance. (Or indicate with which of the people you did start a conversation.)

| PERSON# | ATTRACTIVE QUALITIES | UNATTRACTIVE QUALITIES | REASON TO PURSUE |
|---------|----------------------|------------------------|------------------|
|         |                      |                        |                  |
|         |                      |                        |                  |
|         |                      |                        |                  |
|         |                      |                        |                  |
|         |                      |                        |                  |

## EXERCISE 8.2     KEEPING A BEST FRIEND

**Purpose:**
1.     To determine the reasons you started your best friend relationship.
2.     To understand the reasons you have maintained the friendship.

**Directions:**
1.     Think of your best same-sex friend and your best opposite-sex friend.
2.     List the reasons you became friends with these people.
3.     List the reasons you have maintained friendships with these people.

| Same-sex friend | Initial reasons for the relationship | Current reasons for the relationship |
|---|---|---|
|  |  |  |

| Opposite-sex friend | Initial reasons for the relationship | Current reasons for the relationship |
|---|---|---|
|  |  |  |

**Questions:**
1.     How are the reasons for each of your best friends different?  Similar?

2.     Which initial reasons for the same-sex friendship are still reasons you are friends?

3.     Which initial reasons for the opposite-sex friendship are still reasons you are friends?

# EXERCISE 8.3    LOOKING ATTRACTIVE

**Purpose:**
1.    To become aware of the physical characteristics and qualities that you find attractive.
2.    To identify gender differences in physical attractiveness.

**Directions:**
1.    Make a list of all the physical characteristics you find attractive in males.
2.    Make a list of all the physical characteristics you find attractive in females.

| MALE CHARACTERISTICS | FEMALE CHARACTERISTICS |
| --- | --- |
| | |

**Questions:**

1.    Which characteristics do you find attractive in both males and females?


2.    Which characteristics that you find attractive in others are characteristics that you perceive in yourself?


3.    Which characteristics that you find attractive in others are characteristics that you would like to have, but don't perceive to have yourself?

# EXERCISE 8.4    DISCOVERING SIMILARITIES AND DIFFERENCES

## Purpose:
1.    To discover how similarities and differences in personality, values, cultural background, personal experiences, attitudes, and interests impact your significant relationships.

## Directions:
1.    Think of the most important relationship you have (best friend, spouse, co-worker).
2.    List the similarities you see between you and the other person in each of the categories below.
3.    List the differences you see between you and the other person in each of the categories below.

| CATEGORIES | SIMILARITIES | DIFFERENCES |
|---|---|---|
| Personality | | |
| Values | | |
| Cultural background | | |
| Personal experiences | | |
| Attitudes | | |
| Interests | | |

## Questions:
1.    What impact do your similarities and differences have on your relationship with this person?

# EXERCISE 8.5     EVALUATING NEED COMPATIBILITY

## Purpose:
1. To become aware of your level of need to be included, to be controlled, and to be liked/accepted.
2. To become aware of your level of need to include others, to control others, and to like/accept others.
3. To investigate the compatibility of your needs with the needs of others.
4. To investigate the affect of compatibility of needs on the level of relationships.

## Directions:
1. Evaluate your level of interpersonal needs for each of the following questions by putting your first initial along the rating scale.
2. Ask two close friends to initial along each rating scale to indicate how much each item applies to them.
3. Compare your rating with those of your friends.

---

1. How much do you like to include others in the activities you do?

   Very little 1-----2-----3-----4-----5-----6-----7-----8-----9-----10  A great deal

2. How much do you like to be included by others in activities they are doing?

   Very little 1-----2-----3-----4-----5-----6-----7-----8-----9-----10  A great deal

3. How much do you like to take responsibility for decision making?

   Very little 1-----2-----3-----4-----5-----6-----7-----8-----9-----10  A great deal

4. How much do you like to let others make decisions for you?

   Very little 1-----2-----3-----4-----5-----6-----7-----8-----9-----10  A great deal

5. How much do you feel a need to be accepted and loved by others?

   Very little 1-----2-----3-----4-----5-----6-----7-----8-----9-----10  A great deal

6. How much do you feel a need to accept others and to give love to others?

   Very little 1-----2-----3-----4-----5-----6-----7-----8-----9-----10  A great deal

---

## Questions:
1. In what areas are your needs similar to your friends' needs?
2. In what areas are your needs complementary to your friends' needs?
3. Which matching or differing areas cause difficulties in the relationship, e.g., you both want to make decisions, one wants lots of affection and the other doesn't like to give affection?

Repeat this exercise by choosing two people you know but with whom you probably will not have a close relationship. Follow the same instructions as above.

---

1. How much do you like to include others in the activities you do?

   Very little 1-----2-----3-----4-----5-----6-----7-----8-----9-----10 A great deal

2. How much do you like to be included by others in activities they are doing?

   Very little 1-----2-----3-----4-----5-----6-----7-----8-----9-----10 A great deal

3. How much do you like to take responsibility for decision making?

   Very little 1-----2-----3-----4-----5-----6-----7-----8-----9-----10 A great deal

4. How much do you like to let others make decisions for you?

   Very little 1-----2-----3-----4-----5-----6-----7-----8-----9-----10 A great deal

5. How much do you feel a need to be accepted and loved by others?

   Very little 1-----2-----3-----4-----5-----6-----7-----8-----9-----10 A great deal

6. How much do you feel a need to accept others and to give love to others?

   Very little 1-----2-----3-----4-----5-----6-----7-----8-----9-----10 A great deal

---

## Questions:
1. In what areas are your needs similar to your friends' needs?
2. In what areas are your needs complementary to your friends' needs?
3. Which matching or differing areas cause difficulties in the relationship, e.g., you both want to make decisions, one wants lots of affection and the other doesn't like to give affection?
4. How do similar or complementary needs affect the level of your relationships?

## EXERCISE 8.6    TRACKING ATTRACTION THROUGH COMMUNICATION

**Purpose:**

1.    To determine the level of attraction for people through the amount of communication used.

**Directions:**

1.    Choose four people with whom you interact on a regular basis (neighbors, residence hall neighbors, sorority sisters/fraternity brothers, co-workers).
2.    Using the diagram below, record each contact you have with each person over a three to five day period of time.  You are represented by the center circle.
3.    Draw arrows toward the others' circles each time you initiate conversation.  Mark the arrows with an intersecting line for every subsequent conversation you initiate.
4.    Draw arrows toward your circle each time others initiate conversation with you. Mark the arrows with an intersecting line for every subsequent time they initiate conversation with you.

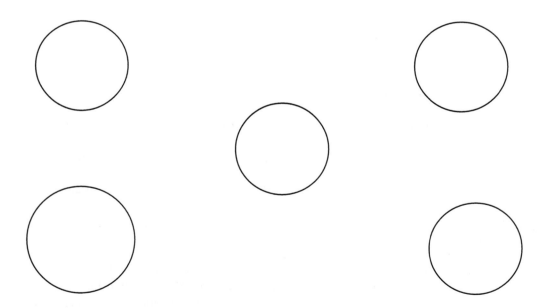

## Questions:

1. With which people do you initiate conversation with most often?  Why?

   _____

   _____

   _____

2. Which people initiate conversation with you most often?  Why?

   _____

   _____

   _____

3. What relationship is there between your level of attraction for the other people and the amount of communication you have with them?  In other words, do you initiate communication with those you find more attractive than with those you do not find as attractive?

   _____

   _____

   _____

   _____

4. What reasons can you give to explain why some people initiate conversation with you more often than you do with them?

   _____

   _____

   _____

   _____

## EXERCISE 8.7    COMPARING ANXIETY AND UNCERTAINTY

**Purpose:**
1.    To determine the relationship between levels of anxiety and levels of familiarity in social situations.

**Directions:**
1.    Write down ten different social situations you can remember in which you participated (refer to the text for ideas).
2.    Indicate your level of nervousness for each situation by putting your initial on the line below.
3.    Indicate your level of familiarity for each situation by initialing the appropriate line.

1.    _____

Calm and cool 1-----2-----3-----4-----5-----6-----7-----8-----9----10   Highly apprehensive

Very familiar  1-----2-----3-----4-----5-----6-----7-----8-----9-----10   Very unfamiliar

2.    _____

Calm and cool 1-----2-----3-----4-----5-----6-----7-----8-----9----10   Highly apprehensive

Very familiar  1-----2-----3-----4-----5-----6-----7-----8-----9-----10   Very unfamiliar

3.    _____

Calm and cool 1-----2-----3-----4-----5-----6-----7-----8-----9----10   Highly apprehensive

Very familiar  1-----2-----3-----4-----5-----6-----7-----8-----9-----10   Very unfamiliar

4.    _____

Calm and cool 1-----2-----3-----4-----5-----6-----7-----8-----9----10   Highly apprehensive

Very familiar  1-----2-----3-----4-----5-----6-----7-----8-----9-----10   Very unfamiliar

5. _____

Calm and cool 1-----2-----3-----4-----5-----6-----7-----8-----9----10   Highly apprehensive

Very familiar  1-----2-----3-----4-----5-----6-----7-----8-----9-----10  Very unfamiliar

6. _____

Calm and cool 1-----2-----3-----4-----5-----6-----7-----8-----9----10   Highly apprehensive

Very familiar  1-----2-----3-----4-----5-----6-----7-----8-----9-----10  Very unfamiliar

7. _____

Calm and cool 1-----2-----3-----4-----5-----6-----7-----8-----9----10   Highly apprehensive

Very familiar  1-----2-----3-----4-----5-----6-----7-----8-----9-----10  Very unfamiliar

8. _____

Calm and cool 1-----2-----3-----4-----5-----6-----7-----8-----9----10   Highly apprehensive

Very familiar  1-----2-----3-----4-----5-----6-----7-----8-----9-----10  Very unfamiliar

9. _____

Calm and cool 1-----2-----3-----4-----5-----6-----7-----8-----9----10   Highly apprehensive

Very familiar  1-----2-----3-----4-----5-----6-----7-----8-----9-----10  Very unfamiliar

10. _____

Calm and cool 1-----2-----3-----4-----5-----6-----7-----8-----9----10   Highly apprehensive

Very familiar  1-----2-----3-----4-----5-----6-----7-----8-----9-----10  Very unfamiliar

## Questions:

1. Which situations were most anxiety producing? Why?

_____

_____

_____

2. To what degree did your unfamiliarity with the situation affect your level of anxiety?

_____

_____

_____

3. What were you most uncertain about in each situation?

_____

_____

_____

4. In which situations were you most comfortable? Why?

_____

_____

_____

5. In which situations, if any, did you feel uncomfortable even though the situation was familiar? Why?

_____

_____

_____

# EXERCISE 8.8     DISCLOSING "ME" TO OTHERS

## Purpose:

1.   To help you identify your level of risk you have in disclosing information about yourself.
2.   To find out how your disclosing behavior relates to that of a significant person in your life

## Directions:

Label each of the statements below, using the following scale:

LR (low risk)  =   you are comfortable disclosing this information to almost anyone

MR (moderate
    risk)   =   you are comfortable disclosing this information to people with whom you have a friendly relationship

HR (high risk) =   you are comfortable disclosing this information only to trustworthy, intimate friends

X   =   you would disclose this information to no one

_____ 1.   Your hobbies, how you like best to spend your spare time
_____ 2.   Your preferences and dislikes in music
_____ 3.   Your educational background and grades
_____ 4.   Your personal views on politics
_____ 5.   Your personal habits that bother you
_____ 6.   Your personal characteristics that make you proud
_____ 7.   Your religious views and your religious participation
_____ 8.   The details of the unhappiest moments of your life
_____ 9.   The details of the happiest moments of your life
_____ 10.  The actions you have regretted most in your life and why
_____ 11.  Your guiltiest secrets
_____ 12.  Your views on the way a husband and wife should live in their marriage
_____ 13.  The main unfulfilled dreams in your life
_____ 14.  What you do, if anything, to stay physically fit
_____ 15.  The aspects of your body you are most pleased with
_____ 16.  The features of your appearance with which you are most displeased
_____ 17.  The person in your life whom you resent most and the reasons why
_____ 18.  The person in your life whom you admire most and the reasons why
_____ 19.  Your most significant fears
_____ 20.  The people with whom you have been sexually intimate and the details about your relationship with each

Give the next survey form to your partner or most significant person in your life.

**Directions:**

Label each of the statements below, using the following scale:

LR (low risk) = you are comfortable disclosing this information to almost anyone

MR (moderate
risk) = you are comfortable disclosing this information to people with whom you have a friendly relationship

HR (high risk) = you are comfortable disclosing this information only to trustworthy, intimate friends

X = you would disclose this information to no one

|  |  |  |
|---|---|---|
| _____ | 1. | Your hobbies, how you like best to spend your spare time |
| _____ | 2. | Your preferences and dislikes in music |
| _____ | 3. | Your educational background and grades |
| _____ | 4. | Your personal views on politics |
| _____ | 5. | Your personal habits that bother you |
| _____ | 6. | Your personal characteristics that make you proud |
| _____ | 7. | Your religious views and your religious participation |
| _____ | 8. | The details of the unhappiest moments of your life |
| _____ | 9. | The details of the happiest moments of your life |
| _____ | 10. | The actions you have regretted most in your life and why |
| _____ | 11. | Your guiltiest secrets |
| _____ | 12. | Your views on the way a husband and wife should live in their marriage |
| _____ | 13. | The main unfulfilled dreams in your life |
| _____ | 14. | What you do, if anything, to stay physically fit |
| _____ | 15. | The aspects of your body you are most pleased with |
| _____ | 16. | The features of your appearance with which you are most displeased |
| _____ | 17. | The person in your life whom you resent most and the reasons why |
| _____ | 18. | The person in your life whom you admire most and the reasons why |
| _____ | 19. | Your most significant fears |
| _____ | 20. | The people with whom you have been sexually intimate and the details about your relationship with each |

**Questions:**

1. What similarities are there between you and your partner in your comfort level of disclosure?
2. What differences are there between you and your partner in your comfort level of disclosure?
3. Which topic areas are you most comfortable disclosing? Why?
4. Which topic areas are you most uncomfortable disclosing? Why are these areas risky for you?
5. How would the differences in your comfort levels of disclosing affect your relationship?

# EXERCISE 8.9    TAKING INVENTORY OF YOUR SELF-DISCLOSURE BEHAVIOR

## Purpose:

1.    To find out your level of comfort and feelings of appropriateness of self-disclosure.

## Directions:

1.    For the list of topics below, identify which information you would share with the following people:

| | | |
|---|---|---|
| A | = | someone you just met |
| B | = | a classmate for the term |
| C | = | an occasional friend |
| D | = | a close friend |
| E | = | a same-sex best friend |
| F | = | an opposite-sex best friend |
| G | = | your mother |
| H | = | your father |

2.    Put the corresponding letter(s) after each topic area.

## TO WHOM WOULD YOU FEEL COMFORTABLE REVEALING YOUR:

1.    HOMETOWN_____

2.    PARENT'S OCCUPATIONS_____

3.    CAREER PLANS_____

4.    INCOME_____

5.    G.P.A._____

6.    REASON FOR
      BREAKING UP WITH
      YOUR LAST MATE_____

7.    GREATEST FEAR_____

8.    PERSONAL RELIGIOUS VIEWS_____

9.    FAVORITE READING MATERIAL_____

10.   TASTE IN CLOTHING_____

11.   GOALS AND AMBITIONS_____

12. FEELINGS ABOUT PEOPLE
    YOU WORK FOR/WITH_____

13. PHYSICAL MEASUREMENTS_____

14. SHOPLIFTING OR CHEATING
    ON AN EXAM/PAPER_____

15. SEX LIFE--PROBLEMS, WITH
    WHOM I HAVE RELATIONS_____

### Questions:

1. Which topics can you share with the most people?  Why?


2. Which topics would you have the most difficulty disclosing?  Why?


3. What might the costs to the relationships be of sharing highly personal information?


4. What might the benefits to the relationships be of sharing personal information?


5. What gender-related conclusions can you make from your inventory?


6. What differences did you observe between the information you would share with your mother and with your father?  Why do these differences exist?

# EXERCISE 8.10    CHOOSING TO AVOID DISCLOSURE

## Purpose:
1.    To identify reasons you do not disclose information to other people.

## Directions:
1.    Choose a particular person with whom you want to analyze your self-disclosing behavior (a close friend, a family member, a co-worker, etc.).
2.    In the column on the left of each item below, indicate the extent to which you use each reason to avoid disclosing:

> 5 = almost always
> 4 = often
> 3 = sometimes
> 2 = rarely
> 1 = never

\_\_\_\_\_    1.    I can't find the opportunity to self-disclose with this person.

\_\_\_\_\_    2.    If I disclose I might hurt the other person.

\_\_\_\_\_    3.    If I disclose I might be evaluating or judging the person.

\_\_\_\_\_    4.    I can't think of topics that I would disclose.

\_\_\_\_\_    5.    Self-disclosure would give information that might be used against me at sometime.

\_\_\_\_\_    6.    If I disclose it might cause me to make personal changes.

\_\_\_\_\_    7.    Self-disclosure might threaten relationships I have with people other than the close acquaintance to whom I disclose.

\_\_\_\_\_    8.    Self-disclosure is a sign of weakness.

\_\_\_\_\_    9.    If I disclose I might lose control over the other person.

\_\_\_\_\_    10.    If I disclose I might discover I am less than I wish to be.

\_\_\_\_\_    11.    If I disclose I might project an image I do not want to project.

\_\_\_\_\_    12.    If I disclose, the other person might not understand what I was saying.

\_\_\_\_\_    13.    If I disclose the other person might evaluate me negatively.

_____ 14.    Self-disclosure is a sign of some emotional disturbance.

_____ 15.    Self-disclosure might hurt our relationship.

_____ 16.    I am afraid that self-disclosure might lead to an intimate relationship with the other person.

_____ 17.    Self-disclosure might threaten my physical safety.

_____ 18.    If I disclose I might give information that makes me appear inconsistent.

_____ 19.    Any other reasons: _____

## Questions:

1.    Which reasons do you use most often to avoid disclosing to this person?




2.    Are the reasons you use most often realistic or legitimate reasons to avoid sharing information with this person?  Why?

# EXERCISE 8.11    DIAGRAMMING DISCLOSURES

## Purpose:
1.    To help you understand the breadth and depth of self-disclosure.
2.    To help you see the differences in the breadth and depth of self-disclosure between types of relationships.

## Directions:
1.    Use the following forms to make social penetration models for three different relationships: an acquaintance, a close same-sex friend, and a close opposite-sex friend.
2.    Identify six topics you might discuss with each person: religion, family, school, hobbies, goals, money, career plans, friendships, etc.
3.    Fill in the pies to indicate which topics you would discuss with each person and to what depth you would share.

The example below shows how to label the pie. You may color in the appropriate areas of the graphs on the next page instead of using arrows.

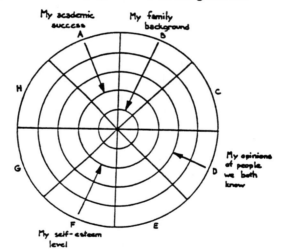

## Questions:

1.    How deep or shallow are your relationships with these people?

2.    Are you satisfied with the depth and breadth of these relationships?

3.    What could you do to change any of these relationships?

ACQUAINTANCE

MALE FRIEND

FEMALE FRIEND

| | |
|---|---|
| Short-term attraction | Long-term maintenance attraction |
| Physical Attraction | Proximity |
| Similarity | Complementarity of Needs |
| Relationship potential | Reciprocation of Liking |
| Communicating Attraction | Affinity Seeking |
| Uncertainty Reduction | Self-disclosure |
| Social Penetration | Johari Window |

| | |
|---|---|
| A liking or positive feeling that motivates us to sustain a relationship. | The degree to which you sense a potential for an interpersonal relationship. |
| That quality which promotes attraction because of being physically close to another and therefore in a position to communicate easily. | Degree to which we find another person's physical self appealing. |
| We are attracted to those whose needs complement our own; one person's weakness is the other person's strength. | We are attracted to people whose personality, values, upbringing, personal experiences, attitudes, and interest are similar to ours. |
| We like people who like us. | We are most attracted to those relationships that potentially have greater rewards or benefits than costs. |
| Strategies used to get other people to like us. | We communicate our attraction toward other people by the use of nonverbal cues, language, and direct declarations. |
| Providing information about ourselves that another person would not learn if we did not tell them. | We seek to reduce our uncertainty about what to expect from other people by attempting to gain information about them. |
| A model of self-disclosure that reflects the movement of information about our self from BLIND, and UNKNOWN quadrants to HIDDEN and OPEN ones. | A model of self-disclosure and relational development that reflects sharing information that has both depth and breadth. |

Approachability Cues

| | Signals from another person that he or she is open to initiating a conversation. |
| --- | --- |

# CHAPTER 9
## ESCALATING, MAINTAINING, AND TERMINATING RELATIONSHIPS

## OBJECTIVES

After studying this chapter in the text, *Interpersonal Communication: Relating to Others*, and completing the exercises in this section of the study guide, you should understand:

1.  the difference between escalating, maintaining, and terminating a relationship,
2.  how to use three strategies for maintaining relationships,
3.  the effect that interpersonal communication skills have on maintaining and escalating relationships,
4.  how ending a relationship follows one of three paths,
5.  the difference between direct and indirect strategies for ending relationships,
6.  the three major causes for breakups,
7.  the elements in Duck's model for ending a relationship, and
8.  how trouble in a relationship is identified through the use of signals

## STUDY QUESTIONS

You should be able to answer the following questions:

1.  What are the three strategies for maintaining interpersonal relationships?
2.  What seven interpersonal skills are associated with maintaining and escalating relationships?
3.  What is the difference between adapting predictively and adapting reactively in a relationship?
4.  What are the adaptation behaviors?
5.  Explain what it means to be rhetorically sensitive?
6.  What are the differences between the Noble Self and the Rhetorical reflector?
7.  What is compliance gaining?
8.  What are the three paths of declining relationships?
9.  What are the indirect and direct strategies for ending relationships?
10. What are the main causes of de-escalation and termination?
11. What are the four phases identified in Duck's model for ending relationships?

# EXERCISE 9.1     SINGING ABOUT RELATIONSHIPS

## Purpose:
1.     To familiarize you with some of the popular sentiments concerning interpersonal relationships as they are expressed in song
2.     To stimulate you to consider the significant concepts and theories in interpersonal relationships by relating them to familiar songs.

## Directions:
1.     Choose a song that expresses a sentiment that is significant to the study of interpersonal relationships because it expresses a sentiment that can assist us in understanding interpersonal relationships.
2.     Choose a song that illustrates a concept or theory that is important in the study of interpersonal relationships.
3.     Choose a song that illustrates a popular relational problem or difficulty.
4.     Choose a song that illustrates a method for dealing with some kind of relationship problem or difficulty.

| NAME OF THE SONG | HOW IT RELATES TO INTERPERSONAL RELATIONSHIPS |
|---|---|
| 1. | |
| 2. | |
| 3. | |
| 4. | |
| 5. | |

# EXERCISE 9.2  ANALYZING INTIMACY IN YOUR RELATIONSHIPS

## Purpose:
1. To determine the level of intimacy in your relationships.
2. To understand the relationship between intimacy and relational maintenance.

## Directions:
1. Choose two important relationships: one with a family member and one with a nonfamily member.
2. Fill out the following surveys, using this scale:

| 5 | 4 | 3 | 2 | 1 |
|---|---|---|---|---|
| Strongly agree | | | | Strongly disagree |

## FAMILY MEMBER:

_____ 1.  The other person and I have a great deal of information about each other.

_____ 2.  The other person and I are highly interdependent.

_____ 3.  The other person and I perform a great many services for each other.

_____ 4.  The other person and I support each other.

_____ 5.  The other person and I understand each other.

_____ 6.  The other person and I satisfy each other's needs, wants, and desires.

_____ 7.  The other person and I accept each other as we are.

_____ 8.  The other person and I avoid hurting each other.

_____  Total score

Examine each answer. The higher your score, the higher the level of intimacy in the relationship and therefore, the greater the possibility that the individual item may be an integral part of the relationship.

Examine the total score. Scores of 32 and above indicate a high degree of intimacy; scores of 20 and below indicate a low degree of intimacy. High scores tend to indicate a relationship that is more fulfilling.

## NONFAMILY MEMBER:

_____ 1.     The other person and I have a great deal of information about each other.

_____ 2.     The other person and I are highly interdependent.

_____ 3.     The other person and I perform a great many services for each other.

_____ 4.     The other person and I support each other.

_____ 5.     The other person and I understand each other.

_____ 6.     The other person and I satisfy each other's needs, wants, and desires.

_____ 7.     The other person and I accept each other as we are.

_____ 8.     The other person and I avoid hurting each other.

_____        Total score

       Examine each answer.  The higher your score, the higher the level of intimacy in the relationship and therefore, the greater the possibility that the individual item may be an integral part of the relationship.

       Examine the total score.  Scores of 32 and above indicate a high degree of intimacy;  scores of 20 and below indicate a low degree of intimacy.  High scores tend to indicate a relationship that is more fulfilling.

## Questions:

1.     In what areas did you have high scores with each person?  How were they similar? Different?
2.     How were your low scores similar or different with each person?
3.     How satisfied are you with the level of intimacy identified?
4.     Have you or the other person ever tried to increase or decrease the level of intimacy?  How did the other person respond?
5.     What behaviors could you use to increase the level of intimacy in the low areas, if you desire to do so?
6.     What behaviors do you engage in to keep the level of intimacy stabilized?
7.     What do your scores tell you about your satisfaction with each relationship?

(Adapted from:  Berko, R.M., Rosenfeld, L.B., & Samovar, L.A. (1994) *Connecting: A Culture-Sensitive Approach to Interpersonal Communication Competency.* Orlando, FL: Harcourt Brace.)

# EXERCISE 9.3     MAINTAINING YOUR RELATIONSHIPS

## Purpose:
1.     To identify the maintenance communication behaviors you use in your relationships.

## Directions:
1.     Choose two people who are not family members with whom you have important relationships.
2.     Briefly describe the relationship with each person.
3.     Comment on each of the strategies for maintaining a relationship listed for each relationship.
4.     Describe how that variable does or does not play a role in the maintenance of your relationship.

| Maintenance Strategy | Person #1 Relationship: | Person #2 Relationship: |
|---|---|---|
| **AVOIDANCE** Ignore things that might change the relationship. | | |
| Avoid doing things that might change the relationship. | | |
| Try to prevent partner from doing things that might change the relationship. | | |

| Maintenance Strategies | Person #1 | Person #2 |
|---|---|---|
| **DIRECTNESS**<br>Directly state that your relationship should remain the same. | | |
| Remind your partner about relationship decisions make in the past. | | |
| Directly tell you partner how you feel about the relationship. | | |
| **BALANCE**<br>Try to maintain a constant level of emotional support. | | |
| Provide favors on a recurring basis for your partner. | | |
| Try to understand your partner's moods and compensate for them. | | |

# EXERCISE 9.4    EXPRESSING EMOTIONS

## Purpose:
1.    To investigate how comfortable you are at expressing emotions in a variety of relationships.

## Directions:
1.    Choose a specific person for each of the following categories:
   a.    a same-sex acquaintance  (SSA)
   b.    an opposite-sex acquaintance (0SA)
   c.    a same-sex friend  (SSF)
   d.    an opposite-sex friend  (OSF)
   e.    a close same-sex friend  (CSSF)
   f.    a close opposite-sex friend (COSF)
   g.    a same-sex parent or relative  (SSP or SSR)
   h.    an opposite-sex parent or relative  (0SP or OSR)
2.    Indicate how comfortable you would be about sharing the following feelings, using the scale below:

Most comfortable                                                                    Least comfortable
   1        2        3        4        5        6        7        8        9        10

| Feeling | SSA | OSA | SSF | OSF | CSSF | COSF | SSP/R | OSP/R |
|---|---|---|---|---|---|---|---|---|
| Liking for the person | | | | | | | | |
| Love for the person | | | | | | | | |
| Anger with the person | | | | | | | | |
| Disap-point-ment with the person | | | | | | | | |
| Liking for a third person | | | | | | | | |
| Love for a third person | | | | | | | | |
| Anger toward a third person | | | | | | | | |

| Disappointment with a third person | | | | | | | | | |
|---|---|---|---|---|---|---|---|---|---|
| Anger toward self | | | | | | | | | |
| Disappointment in self | | | | | | | | | |
| embarrassment | | | | | | | | | |
| Your fears | | | | | | | | | |
| Happy | | | | | | | | | |
| Excitement | | | | | | | | | |
| Pride | | | | | | | | | |
| Uncertainty | | | | | | | | | |

## Questions:

1.     With whom are you most comfortable sharing your emotions?


2.     Which emotions are you most open about?


3.     Which emotions are you most closed about?


4.     What makes you uncomfortable about sharing certain emotions?


5.     Which emotions do you consider to be negative feelings? Positive?

**EXERCISE 9.5      RECOGNIZING YOUR EMOTIONS**

<u>**Purpose**</u>:
1.  To help you identify the emotions you experience.
2.  To help you identify how you deal with your emotions.
3.  To make you aware of how your emotions affect you and your relationships.

<u>**Directions**</u>:
1.  Observe your thoughts, feelings, and behaviors for several days.
2.  Fill in the appropriate spaces on the form below.

| Emotion(s) | Who is involved? In what circumstances? | How did you recognize the emotions? | What did you do? (Verbally and nonverbally) | What effect was there for you and others? |
|---|---|---|---|---|
| 1. | | | | |
| 2. | | | | |
| 3. | | | | |

| 4. | | | | |
|----|----|----|----|----|
| 5. | | | | |

**Questions:**

1. What emotions do you feel most often?  In what circumstances and with what people?

2. How do you recognize you emotions?

3. In what ways do you deal with your emotions?

4. How does your emotional state affect your behavior?

5. How does your emotional behavior affect your relationships with others?

6. In what ways would you like to change your emotional communication behaviors?

(Adapted from:  Wiemann, M.O. & Adler, R.B. (1984) *Looking Out, Looking In Activities Manual*. New York, NY: Holt, Rinehart, and Winston.)

# EXERCISE 9.6    COMMUNICATING WITH SENSITIVITY

## Purpose:
1.    To help you become aware of your communication sensitivity.

## Directions:
1.    For each of the following items, decide whether you feel the item is:

| 1 | 2 | 3 |
|---|---|---|
| Almost always true | Sometimes true | Almost never true |

_____    1.    A person should tell it like it is.

_____    2.    You should tell someone if you think he or she is giving you bad advice.

_____    3.    Saying what you think is a sign of friendship.

_____    4.    It is better to speak your gut feelings than to beat around the bush.

_____    5.    When someone has an irritating habit, he or she should be told about it.

_____    6.    If people would open up to each other, the world would be a better place.

## Scoring:

1.    Count the number of 1's you marked. This corresponds to the Noble Self communicators.
2.    Count the number of 2's you marked. This corresponds to the Rhetorically Sensitive communicators.
3.    Count the number of 3's you marked. This corresponds to the Rhetorical Reflectors.

## Questions:
1.    What do your responses indicate about you?

2.    How do they match with your own perception of yourself?

3.    How does your classification affect the way you communicate with others?

4.    If your score indicated a low Rhetorically Sensitive communicator, what could you change about your communication behavior to become more sensitive.

**EXERCISE 9.7      ENDING YOUR RELATIONSHIPS**

**Purpose:**
1.      To become aware of how and why relationships end.
2.      To determine which strategies you use when ending a relationship.
3.      To investigate the reasons your relationships ended.

**Directions:**
1.      Think of two relationships (friendships) that you once had, but you have now terminated.
2.      Fill out the form below with information about the ending of each relationship.

RELATIONSHIP #1

Describe the relationship _____

_____

What type of ending did your relationship have?  (Circle one of the choices below)

         Faded away           Sudden death          Incrementalism

Explain why the relationship ended the way it did. _____

_____

Which of the following strategies did you use to end the relationship?

         Withdrawal          Pseudo de-escalation          Cost escalation

Negative Identity    Management    Justification    De-escalation    Positive Tone

How did your partner react to the strategy(ies)?_____

_____

How did you feel using the strategy(ies)?_____

_____

Why did you end the relationship?_____

_____

_____

RELATIONSHIP #2

Describe the relationship _____

_____

What type of ending did your relationship have?  (Circle one of the choices below)

        Faded away        Sudden death        Incrementalism

Explain why the relationship ended the way it did. _____

_____

Which of the following strategies did you use to end the relationship?

       Withdrawal       Pseudo de-escalation       Cost escalation

Negative Identity    Management    Justification    De-escalation    Positive Tone

How did your partner react to the strategy(ies)?_____

_____

How did you feel using the strategy(ies)?_____

_____

Why did you end the relationship?_____

_____

_____

**Questions:**
1.    What differences were there in how the relationships ended?
2.    What effects do you think the choice of strategy had on you and your partner?
3.    What effects do you think the choice of strategy had on the type of ending the relationship had?
4.    How satisfied were you with the ending of each of these relationships?
5.    If you could do it over again, what would you do differently?  Why?

| | |
|---|---|
| Avoidance | Directness |
| Balance | Adaptation |
| Predictive Adaptation | Reactive Adaptation |
| Communication Sensitivity | Rhetorical Sensitivity |
| Noble Self | Rhetorical Reflector |
| Conversational Sensitivity | Nonverbal Sensitivy |

| | |
|---|---|
| A strategy for maintaining a relationship that involves coming out and saying you want things to remain the same. | A strategy for maintaining a relationship that involves ignoring discussions or opportunities for redefining the relationship. |
| Adjusting your behavior in accordance with the relationship or situation. | A strategy for maintaining a relationship that involves providing enough support to keep the relationship at a particular level. |
| Adjusting your behavior in response to another's behavior or to an event. | Adjusting your behavior in anticipation of another's reaction or of an event. |
| A willingness and ability to adapt combined with a sensitivity and perceptiveness about your own self, the situation, and the other. | An awareness and appreciation of all the dynamics of interpersonal interactions. |
| An individual who overadapts, taking on a self to fit each situation. | An individual who is inflexible and refuses to adapt because he or she thinks that would be hypocritical. |
| The ability to pick up and accurately interpret nonverbal cues. | The ability to pick up meanings in what is said, remember what was said, and compose multiple ways of saying the same thing. |

| | |
|---|---|
| Compliance Gaining | Relational De-escalation |
| Bilateral Dissolution | Unilateral Dissolution |
| Fading Away | Sudden Death |
| Incrementalism | Indirect Relational Termination Strategies |
| Direct Relational Termination Strategies | Intra-Psychic Phase |
| Dyadic Phase | Social Phase |

| | |
|---|---|
| The downward movement of a relationship from one level to another through the reduction of intimacy, commitment, self-disclosing, and general resources. | The use of persuasive strategies to accomplish interpersonal goals. |
| Ending a relationship when only one party is agreeable. | Ending a relationship when both parties are agreeable. |
| Ending a relationship abruptly and with preparation. | Ending a relationship by slowly drifting apart. |
| Attempts to break up a relationship without explicitly stating the desire to do so. | Ending a relationship when conflicts and problems finally reach a critical mass. |
| The first phase in a model of relationship termination: an individual engages in an internal evaluation of the partner | Explicit statements of a desire to break up a relationship. |
| The third phase in a model of relationship termination: the social network around both parties are informed and become involved | The second phase in a model of relationship termination: the individual discusses termination with the partner. |

Grave Dressing Phase

| | The final phase in a model relationship termination: the partners generate public explanations and move past the relationship. |
|---|---|

# CHAPTER 10
## MANAGING CONFLICT IN INTERPERSONAL RELATIONSHIPS

## OBJECTIVES

After studying the material in this chapter of *Interpersonal Communication: Relating to Others* and completing the exercises in this section of the study guide, you should understand:

1. how the definition of conflict relates to interpersonal communication,
2. the differences between the three types of interpersonal conflict,
3. the source of the commonly held myths about interpersonal conflict,
4. the differences between destructive and constructive approaches to conflict management,
5. the functions of the five stages of conflict,
6. how the five types of power relate to interpersonal conflict,
7. the basic elements of three types of conflict management styles, and
8. what to do to manage your emotions, information, goals, and problems in a conflict situations.

## STUDY QUESTIONS

You should be able to answer the following questions:

1. What is conflict?
2. How are pseudo conflict, simple conflict, and ego conflict the same and different?
3. What are the commonly held myths about interpersonal conflict and where did they originate?
4. What is the difference between the destructive and constructive approaches to managing conflict?
5. Describe the five stages of conflict and explain the communication behaviors that occur in each stage.
6. What are the five different types of power? How do they relate to conflict?
7. What are the three types of conflict management styles and what communication behaviors are exhibited with each style?
8. What conflict management skills can you use to manage your emotions, information, goals, and problems when trying to resolve interpersonal differences?

# EXERCISE 10.1    IDENTIFYING GOALS IN CONFLICT SITUATIONS

## Purpose:
1.    To help you learn to identify goals in conflict situations.
2.    To help you understand how the perception of different goals leads to conflict.

## Directions:
1.    Make a list of the conflicts you have been involved in during the last week.
2.    Identify what your goals were in each conflict.
3.    Write down the goals the other person had in each situation.

| Participants | Your goals | Other's goals | How the conflict was acted out |
|---|---|---|---|
| 1. | | | |
| 2. | | | |
| 3. | | | |
| 4. | | | |

## EXERCISE 10.2    WATCHING CONFLICT DIVERSITY

**Purpose:**

1.    To help you recognize cultural differences in conflict situations.

**Directions:**

1.    Watch a movie or a television show in which different cultures are represented (gender, age, nationality, etc.)--*Joy Luck Club, When a Man Loves a Woman, Roseanne, Northern Exposure* are examples that might work.
2.    Observe the behavior of the actors in conflict situations.
3.    Using the information in Chapter 10 in the text, record any differences in behavior that you notice.

Name the show: _____

Describe the participants: _____

_____

_____

Describe the conflict situation: _____

_____

_____

Describe the gender differences: (if applicable) _____

_____

_____

Describe the cultural differences: (if applicable) _____

_____

_____

**Questions:**

1.    Do you think the conflict you observed was a true representation of "typical" conflict behavior for the cultures involved?  Why or why not?
2.    How did the conflict behaviors compare to the information in Chapter 10 of your text?

# EXERCISE 10.3 CATEGORIZING CONFLICT TYPES

## Purpose:
1. To help you learn the differences between the three types of conflict--pseudo conflict, simple conflict, and ego conflict.
2. To learn to recognize the communication behaviors used in each conflict type.

## Directions:
1. For each type of conflict, give an example from your experiences or observations of other people in conflict.
2. Describe the communication behaviors for each type of conflict that led you to choose the conflict to represent each type.

## PSEUDO CONFLICT:

Description of a pseudo conflict: _____

_____

_____

Communication behaviors used by each participant: _____

_____

Outcome of the conflict: _____

_____

## SIMPLE CONFLICT:

Description of a simple conflict: _____

_____

_____

Communication behaviors used by each participant: _____

_____

Outcome of the conflict: _____

_____

## EGO CONFLICT:

Description of an ego conflict: _____

_____

_____

Communication behaviors used by each participant: _____

_____

Outcome of the conflict: _____

_____


## **Questions:**

1.    Which type of conflict was most difficult for you to find an example of?

2.    Which type of conflict do you have most in your interpersonal relationships?

3.    How did the communication behaviors affect the outcome of the conflicts?

4.    What could have been done differently to change the outcome (if the outcome was not satisfactory to the participants)?

# EXERCISE 10.4    MOVING THROUGH THE STAGES OF CONFLICT

## Purpose:

1.    To help you recognize how conflict moves through the stages of prior conditions, frustration awareness, active, resolution, and follow up stages.
2.    To become aware of the communication behaviors used during each stage.

## Directions:

1.    Think about a recent conflict that you have had or are having and trace its development through the stages of conflict escalation.
2.    If it is a conflict that hasn't been resolved, plot the evolution of the conflict to its current stage and consider some possible solutions for the conflict.
3.    Identify the communication behaviors you and your partner used in each stage.

---

1.    Prior condition's stage: What was the source of the conflict? What communication       behaviors were used?

2.    Frustration awareness stage: When and how did you become aware of the conflict? What communication behaviors were used?

3.    Resolution: Is there a solution. If so, what is it? If not, what are some ways the conflict could be managed? What communication behaviors were used?

4.    Follow up: Is the conflict over? Do you still harbor some resentment? If so, what are strategies to help you manage the resentment? What communication behaviors were used?

# EXERCISE 10.5    CHECKING POWER BALANCE

## Purpose:
1.    To become aware of your perception of power in a conflict situation.

## Directions:
1.    Think of a conflict in which you are involved at the present time.
2.    Rate your own power and the power of your partner in relation to the conflict.
3.    If possible, also give your partner a copy of the survey so you can compare your perceptions about power in your conflict.

Fill out the survey below according to the following:

| | | |
|---|---|---|
| 3 | = | High power |
| 2 | = | Medium power |
| 1 | = | Low power |

| Self | | Other |
|---|---|---|
| | *Self* | *Other* |
| _____ | Legitimate Power (Position) | _____ |
| _____ | Referent Power (Reputation) | _____ |
| _____ | Coercive Power (Ability to Punish) | _____ |
| _____ | Reward Power (Resource Control) | _____ |
| _____ | Expert Power (Knowledge and Skill) | _____ |
| _____ | TOTALS | _____ |

Scoring:  If your total power score and that of your partner are within 4 points of each other, you are in an equal-power situation.  A difference greater than 4 points suggests an unequal balance of power.

Ask your partner to fill out the copy of the survey on the next page.  Compare your perceptions of power in this conflict situation.

Fill out the survey below according to the following:

| | | |
|---|---|---|
| 3 | = | High power |
| 2 | = | Medium power |
| 1 | = | Low power |

| Self | | Other |
|---|---|---|
| _____ | Legitimate Power (Position) | _____ |
| _____ | Referent Power (Reputation) | _____ |
| _____ | Coercive Power (Ability to Punish) | _____ |
| _____ | Reward Power (Resource Control) | _____ |
| _____ | Expert Power (Knowledge and Skill) | _____ |
| _____ | TOTALS | _____ |

Scoring: If your total power score and that of your partner are within 4 points of each other, you are in an equal-power situation. A difference greater than 4 points suggests an unequal balance of power.

## Questions:

1.  In what types of power were your perceptions similar to your partner? Which types were different?

2.  If you have a power imbalance, what can you do to equalize the power?

3.  How is the power distribution contributing to the conflict situation?

This exercise is reproduced for student use from the text, *Interpersonal Communication: Relating to Others.*

# EXERCISE 10.6    IDENTIFYING YOUR CONFLICT STRATEGIES

## Purpose:
1.    To help you increase your awareness of the conflict strategies you use.

## Directions:
1.    Think of situations in which you find yourself differing from those of another person.
2.    In the following survey, circle the **A** or **B** statement that is ***most characteristic*** of your behavior.  If neither answer is very typical of your behavior, select the response that you would be ***more likely*** to use.

---

1.    A    There are times when I let others take responsibility for solving the problem.
      B    Rather than negotiate the things on which we disagree, I try to stress those things upon which we both agree.

2.    A    I try to find a compromise solution.
      B    I attempt to deal with all of the other person's and my concerns.

3.    A    I am usually firm in pursuing my goals.
      B    I might try to soothe the other's feelings and preserve our relationship.

4.    A    I try to find a compromise solution.
      B    I sometimes sacrifice my own wishes for the wishes of the other person.

5.    A    I consistently seek the other's help in working out a solution.
      B    I try to do what is necessary to avoid useless tensions.

6.    A    I try to avoid creating unpleasantness for myself.
      B    I try to win my position.

7.    A    I try to postpone the issue until I have had some time to think it over.
      B    I give up some points in exchange for others.

8.    A    I am usually firm is pursuing my goals.
      B    I attempt to get all concerns and issues immediately out in the open.

9.    A    I feel that differences are not always worth worrying about.
      B    I make some effort to get my way.

10.   A    I am firm in pursuing my goals.
      B    I try to find a compromise solution.

11.     A      I attempt to get all concerns and issues immediately out in the open.
           B      I might try to soothe the other's feelings and preserve our relationship.

12.     A      I sometimes avoid taking positions which would create controversy.
           B      I will let the other person have some of his/her positions if the person lets me have some of mine.

13.     A      I propose a middle ground.
           B      I press to get my points made.

14.     A      I tell the other person my ideas and ask for his/hers.
           B      I try to show the other person the logic and benefits of my position.

15.     A      I might try to soothe the other's feelings and preserve our relationship.
           B      I try to do what is necessary to avoid tensions.

Circle the letters below which you circled on each item of the questionnaire.

| | D | I | C | A | S |
|---|---|---|---|---|---|
| 1. | | | | A | B |
| 2. | | B | A. | | |
| 3. | A | | | | B |
| 4. | | | A | | B |
| 5. | | A | | B | |
| 6. | B | | | A | |
| 7. | | | B | A | |
| 8. | A | B | | | |
| 9. | B | | | A | |
| 10. | A | | B | | |
| 11. | | A | | | B |
| 12. | | | B | A | |
| 13. | B | | A | | |
| 14. | B | A | | | |
| 15. | | | | B | A |

Record your scores as follows:

The number of **A**s and **B**s circled in column D (Dominance or Controlling) _____
The number of **A**s and **B**s circled in column I (Integration or Cooperative) _____
The number of **A**s and **B**s circled in column C (Compromise) _____
The number of **A**s and **B**s circled in column A (Avoidance or Withdraw) _____
The number of **A**s and **B**s circled in column S (Smoothing or Placating) _____

**Questions:**

1.    On which of the five strategies did you score highest? Lowest?

2.    How often do you use the strategy that you scored highest?

3.    In what situations do you use that strategy? How do you decide which strategy to use?

(Adapted from: Berko, et al. (1994) *Connecting: A Culture-sensitive Approach to Interpersonal Communication Competency.* Orlando, FL: Harcourt Brace.)

# EXERCISE 10.7    ANALYZING YOUR CONFLICT COMMUNICATION

## Purpose:
1.    To become aware of your use of nonassertive, assertive, and aggressive communication behavior in conflict situations.

## Directions:

Indicate, on a scale of 1 to 7, the degree to which each of the following statements describes your conflict communication behavior. Use the following scale:

| | | | | | |
|---|---|---|---|---|---|
| 1 | = | Never | 5 | = | Often |
| 2 | = | Very seldom | 6 | = | Very often |
| 3 | = | Seldom | 7 | = | Always |
| 4 | = | Sometimes | | | |

_____    1.    I blend ideas with others to create new solutions to conflict.

_____    2.    I shy away from topics that are sources of disputes.

_____    3.    I strongly insist on my position being accepted during a conflict.

_____    4.    I try to find solutions that combine a variety of viewpoints.

_____    5.    I steer clear of disagreeable situations.

_____    6.    I give in to other people's ideas.

_____    7.    I look for middle-of-the-road solutions that satisfy both my needs and the needs of the other person.

_____    8.    I avoid a person I suspect of wanting to discuss a disagreement.

_____    9.    I minimize the significance of a conflict.

_____    10.    I build an integrated solution from the issues raised in a dispute.

_____    11.    I stress a point I am making by hitting my fist on the table when I insist the other person is wrong.

_____    12.    I argue insistently for my position and needs.

_____    13.    I shout when trying to get others to accept my position.

_____    14.    I look for mutually satisfying creative solutions to conflicts.

_____ 15. I keep quiet about my views in order to avoid disagreements.

_____ 16. I dominate arguments until others accept my ideas.

_____ 17. I'm willing to give in a little if the other person will consider my needs.

_____ 18. I assert my opinions forcefully.

SCORING:

Add your scores for questionnaire items numbered:
2, 5, 6, 8, 9, 15: _____

This is your score for *nonassertiveness*. A high numerical score (35 or above) means you use this style of communication often. A low numerical score (13 or below) means you seldom use this style.

Add your scores for items numbered:
1, 4, 7, 10, 14, 17: _____

This is your *assertiveness* score. A high numerical score (35 or above) means you tend to use this style of communication often. A low numerical score (13 or below) means you seldom use this style.

Add your scores for items numbered:
3, 11, 12, 13, 16, 18: _____

This is your *aggressiveness* score. A high numerical score (35 or above) means you tend to use this style of communication often. A low numerical score (13 or below) means you seldom use this style.

Compare your scores on the three dimensions to see which style of communication you use most and least often in conflict situations.

## Questions:
1. Which communication behaviors do you tend to use most often in conflict situations?
2. Which behaviors do you use least often?
3. In what conflict situations do you use your most often used behaviors?
4. In what relationships do you tend to use nonassertiveness, assertiveness, and aggressiveness?
5. How satisfied are you with the results of this questionnaire?
6. What can you do to change your communication behaviors, if you are not satisfied?

(This exercise was adapted from Wilmot, W., Hocker, J., & Clairmont, L. (1991) *Interpersonal Conflict: Instructor's Manual*. Dubuque, IA: Brown.)

## EXERCISE 10.8    FOCUSING YOUR CONFLICT THOUGHTS

**Purpose:**

1.    To learn to focus your conflicts on wants, needs, and have-to-haves.

**Directions:**

1.    Think of three of your most serious, important conflicts.
2.    Determine what you want, need, and have to have out of each conflict.


CONFLICT #1

Describe the conflict: _____

_____

_____


Complete the following statements:

What I **WANT** out of this situation is: _____

_____

What I **NEED** out of this situation is:  _____

_____

What I **HAVE TO HAVE** out of this situation is: _____

_____


CONFLICT #2

Describe the conflict: _____

_____

_____

Complete the following statements:

What I **WANT** out of this situation is: _____

_____

What I **NEED** out of this situation is: _____

_____

What I **HAVE TO HAVE** out of this situation is: _____

_____


CONFLICT #3

Describe the conflict: _____

_____

_____


Complete the following statements:

What I **WANT** out of this situation is:_____

_____

What I **NEED** out of this situation is: _____

_____

What I **HAVE TO HAVE** out of this situation is: _____

_____

## Questions:

1.  Which was more difficult to determine--your wants, your needs, or your have-to-haves in each conflict? Why?
2.  How did the issue of the conflicts affect your choices?
3.  How did the relationship with the other person affect your choices?

# EXERCISE 10.9    DESCRIBING YOUR CONFLICTS

## Purpose:
1.    To learn to look at both sides of a conflict situation.

## Directions:
1.    During the next week, choose three conflicts to analyze. These conflicts do not have to be major conflicts, but simply situations where you and another person are preventing one or the other from achieving a goal.
2.    Describe the conflict in terms of who it was with, what it was about, when it occurred, what the outcome was, how it was resolved, etc.
3.    Describe your perspective--what you saw as the problem and the cause, how you behaved, how you felt, how you think the other person behaved.
4.    Try to decenter and describe the conflict from the other person's perspective, by looking at what they would say the problem was, what the cause was, how they think you behaved, how they felt, how they would describe their behavior.

## CONFLICT #1

Describe the conflict: _____

_____

_____

Your perspective of the conflict: _____

_____

_____

Your interpretation of the other person's perspective: _____

_____

_____

Optional: The other person's actual perception: _____

_____

_____

What you discovered by comparing perspectives: _____

_____

**CONFLICT #2**

Describe the conflict: _____

_____

_____

Your perspective of the conflict: _____

_____

_____

Your interpretation of the other person's perspective: _____

_____

_____

Optional: The other person's actual perception: _____

_____

_____

What you discovered by comparing perspectives: _____

_____

**CONFLICT #3**

Describe the conflict: _____

_____

_____

Your perspective of the conflict: _____

_____

_____

Your interpretation of the other person's perspective: _____

_____

_____

Optional: The other person's actual perception: _____

_____

_____

What you discovered by comparing perspectives: _____

_____

| Conflict | Expressive Conflict |
|---|---|
| Instrumental Conflict | Pseudo Conflict |
| Simple Conflict | Ego Conflict |
| Conflict Myths | Constructive Conflict |
| Destructive Conflict | Power |
| Legitimate Power | Referent Power |

| | |
|---|---|
| Conflict that focuses on issues about the quality of the relationship and managing interpersonal tension and hostility. | A struggle that occurs when two people cannot agree upon a way to meet their needs or goals. |
| Conflict triggered by a lack of understanding and miscommunication. | Conflict that centers on achieving a particular goal or task and less on relational issues. |
| Conflict that is based upon personal issues; conflicting partners attack one another's self esteem. | Conflict that stems from different ideas, definitions, perceptions, or goals. |
| Conflict that helps build new insights and establishes new patterns in a relationship. | Inappropriate assumptions about the nature of interpersonal conflict. |
| The resources an individual has to influence another person. | Conflict that dismantles relationships without restoring the relationship. |
| Influence based upon being well liked and respected. | Influence based upon being appointed, elected or selected by someone to exercise control. |

| Expert Power | Reward Power |
| --- | --- |
| Coercive Power | Sexual Harassment |
| Non-confrontational Style | Controlling Style |
| Cooperative Style | Assertiveness |
| Agressiveness | |

| | |
|---|---|
| Influence based upon a person's ability to provide positive rewards and favors. | Influence based upon knowledge and experience that an individual possesses. |
| Unwanted sexual advances, requests for sexual favors, or other inappropriate verbal or physical behavior of a sexual nature | Influence based upon someone's ability to punish another person. |
| A style of managing conflict motivated by a desire to dominate. Behaviors include blaming, threatening, warning and other forms of verbal abuse. | A style of managing conflict that includes placing, distracting, computing, withdrawing, and giving in. |
| Pursuing your best interests without denying your partner's rights. | A style of managing conflict that seeks win-win solutions to problems. Cooperative people separate the people from the problem, focus on shared interests, generate multiple solutions, and base decisions on objective criteria. |
| | Expressing your interests while denying the rights of others by blaming, judging and evaluating the other person. |

# CHAPTER 11
## INTERPERSONAL COMMUNICATION AND CULTURAL DIVERSITY

## OBJECTIVES

After studying the material in this chapter of *Interpersonal Communication: Relating to Others* and completing the exercises in this section of the study guide, you should understand:

1.  the meaning of culture and cultural diversity,
2.  the difference between cultural elements, cultural values, cultural goals, and cultural contexts,
3.  the difference between enculturation and acculturation,
4.  the main aspects of the dimensions of cultural values,
5.  the difference between high-context and low-context cultures,
6.  the difference in the verbal and nonverbal communication behaviors in different cultures,
7.  the impact of ethnocentrism, different communication codes, stereotyping and prejudice, and assumptions of similarity on intercultural communication, and
8.  the strategies to use to communicate effectively in intercultural situations.

## STUDY QUESTIONS

You should be able to answer the following questions:

1.  What is culture?
2.  How do cultural elements, values, goals, and contexts make up our cultural identity?
3.  What is the difference between enculturation and acculturation?
4.  What are the four variables that measure values in almost every culture?
5.  What is meant by masculine and feminine cultures?
6.  What is the difference between high-context and low context cultures and what countries are examples of each?
7.  What is ethnocentrism?
8.  How do cultural stereotypes and prejudice affect interpersonal communication?
9.  How do marriage customs vary from one culture to another?
10. What can we do to close the communication gap between cultures?

## EXERCISE 11.1    IDENTIFYING INTERCULTURAL INFLUENCES

**Purpose:**
1.    To become aware of the many cultural influences in your daily life.

**Directions:**
1.    Identify the intercultural encounters you have had during the past week.
2.    Use the space below to organize your experiences.

Friends or family members who are from a culture other than my own:

_____    _____

_____    _____

_____    _____

People I have met from a culture other than my own:

_____    _____

_____    _____

_____    _____

_____    _____

Ethnic foods I have eaten (not counting pizza):

_____    _____

_____    _____

_____    _____

_____    _____

Situations in which I heard someone speaking a language other than my own:

1. _____

2. _____

3. _____

# EXERCISE 11.2    ASSESSING YOUR COMMUNICATION WITH STRANGERS

## Purpose:
1.    To identify your comfort level in communicating with strangers and people from other cultures.

## Directions:
1.    Respond to each statement below by indicating the degree to which it is true of your communication with strangers.
2.    Use the following scale for your responses:

|   |   |   |
|---|---|---|
| 1 | = | Always False |
| 2 | = | Usually False |
| 3 | = | Sometimes True/Sometimes False |
| 4 | = | Usually True |
| 5 | = | Always True |

_____    1.    I accept strangers as they are.

_____    2.    I express my feelings when I communicate with strangers.

_____    3.    I avoid negative stereotyping when I communicate with strangers.

_____    4.    I find similarities between my self and strangers when we communicate.

_____    5.    I accommodate my behavior to strangers when we communicate.


Add the numbers you wrote next to each statement. Scores range from 5 to 25. The higher your score, the greater your potential is for developing a strong relationship with someone from a different background.

This exercise is reproduced for student use from the text, *Interpersonal Communication: Relating to Others.*

## EXERCISE 11.3    DEVELOPING CULTURAL ELEMENTS

**Purpose:**
1.    To become aware of how you learned the cultural elements that influence you.
2.    To become aware of how you learned new cultural elements.

**Directions:**
1.    Give an example for each of the following cultural elements that you have had for most of your life.  Tell how you learned to value each.
2.    List a newly acquired or learned example for each of the cultural elements. Tell how you learned to value each.

---

**ENCULTURATION EXAMPLES:**

Material culture--a thing or an idea:

_____

_____

Social institutions--a school, government office, religious organization:

_____

_____

Individuals and the universe--a belief:

_____

_____

Aesthetics--a type of music, theater, art, dance:

_____

_____

Language--verbal and nonverbal communication pattern:

_____

## ACCULTURATION EXAMPLES:

Material culture--a thing or an idea:

_____

_____

Social institutions--a school, government office, religious organization:

_____

_____

Individuals and the universe--a belief:

_____

_____

Aesthetics--a type of music, theater, art, dance:

_____

_____

Language--verbal and nonverbal communication pattern:

_____

_____

# EXERCISE 11.4    PLACING VALUE ON CULTURAL DIMENSIONS

## Purpose:
1.    To understand how you learned your cultural values.
2.    To determine changes in your values.

## Directions:
1.    For each of the following dimensions of cultural values, identify those that you were raised with.
2.    Describe how your values affected your communication and relationships with people from cultures other than the one you were raised in.

## DIMENSION

Masculine vs. Feminine

Values you were raised with: _____

_____

Effect on relationships: _____

_____

Individual vs. Group

Values you were raised with: _____

_____

Effect on relationships: _____

_____

Tolerance for Uncertainty vs. Need for Certainty

Values you were raised with: _____

_____

Effect on relationships: _____

_____

## Concentrated vs. Decentralized Power

Values you were raised with: _____

_____

Effects on relationships:

_____

_____

# EXERCISE 11.5 DISCOVERING BARRIERS TO CULTURAL COMMUNICATION

**Purpose:**

1. To become aware of the barriers that inhibit effective intercultural communication.

**Directions:**

1. For each barrier listed below, describe two examples you have encountered or observed in your experiences.
2. Discuss how the example you give interfered with effective communication.

## BARRIER

Ethnocentrism

1. Example encountered: _____

   _____

   Impact on communication: _____

   _____

2. Example encountered: _____

   _____

   Impact on communication: _____

   _____

Different Communication Codes

1. Example encountered: _____

   _____

   Impact on communication: _____

   _____

2. Example encountered: _____

   _____

Impact on communication: _____

_____

## Stereotyping and Prejudice

1. Example encountered: _____

_____

     Impact on communication: _____

_____

2. Example encountered: _____

_____

     Impact on communication: _____

_____

## Assuming Similarity

1. Example encountered: _____

_____

     Impact on communication: _____

_____

2. Example encountered: _____

_____

     Impact on communication: _____

_____

## EXERCISE 11.6     MINDING YOUR MANNERS

**Purpose:**

1.      To help you understand rules and manners for people in the United States.
2.      To learn that expectations for manners differ from person to person within the same culture.

**Directions:**

1.      Identify appropriate rules for behavior in the following situations.
2.      Ask two other people to fill out the questionnaire--friends, family members, or co-workers.
3.      Compare the responses.

You fill out this questionnaire:

Expectations regarding punctuality at meetings: _____

_____

How good friends greet one another: _____

_____

How business or professional colleagues greet one another: _____

_____

Gift giving and receiving etiquette among friends: _____

_____

Gift giving and receiving etiquette among business associates: _____

_____

Typical times for daily meals: _____

_____

When use of someone's first name is appropriate: _____

_____

When use of someone's first name is not appropriate: _____

_____

Have another person fill out this questionnaire:

Expectations regarding punctuality at meetings: _____

How good friends greet one another: _____

How business or professional colleagues greet one another: _____

Gift giving and receiving etiquette among friends: _____

Gift giving and receiving etiquette among business associates: _____

Typical times for daily meals: _____

When use of someone's first name is appropriate: _____

When use of someone's first name is not appropriate: _____

-------------------------------------------------------------------------------------

Have another person fill out this questionnaire:

Expectations regarding punctuality at meetings: _____

How good friends greet one another: _____

How business or professional colleagues greet one another: _____

Gift giving and receiving etiquette among friends: _____

Gift giving and receiving etiquette among business associates: _____

Typical times for daily meals: _____

When use of someone's first name is appropriate: _____

When use of someone's first name is not appropriate: _____

**Questions:**

1.     Which rules for manners are the most similar on the questionnaire responses?

2.     Which rules are different?

3.     What does this suggest about how reliable the suggestions are for people from other countries who are trying to learn effective communication behaviors in the U.S.?

| Culture | Co-culture |
|---------|------------|
| Cultural Elements | Enculturation |
| Cultural Values | Masculine Cultural Values |
| Feminine Cultural Values | Cultural Goals |
| Cultural Context | High Context Culture |
| Low Context Culture | Ethnocentrism |

| | |
|---|---|
| A culture that exists within a larger cultural context (e.g. the gay and lesbian culture). | A learned system of knowledge, behavior, attitudes, beliefs, values, and norms that is shared by a group of people. |
| The process of communicating a group's culture from generation to generation. | Categories of things and ideas that identify the most profound aspects of cultural influence (e.g. schools, governments, music, theater, language). |
| A masculine culture values achievement, assertiveness, heroism, and material wealth. | What a given group of people values or appreciates. |
| A culture's objectives in terms of individual or collective achievement. | A feminine culture values relationships, caring for the less fortunate, and overall quality of life. |
| A culture that derives much information from nonverbal and environmental cues. | Information not explicitly communicated through language, such as environmental or nonverbal cues. |
| The belief that your cultural traditions and assumptions are superior to others. | A culture that derives much information from the words of a message and less information from nonverbal and environmental cues. |

| | |
|---|---|
| Stereotype | Prejudice |
| Intercultural Communication | Culture Shock |
| World View | |

| | |
|---|---|
| Pre-judging someone before you know all of the facts or background of that person. | To place a person or group of persons into an inflexible, all-encompassing category. |
| The feeling of stress and anxiety a person experiences when encountering a culture different from his or her own. | Communication between or among people who have different cultural traditions. |
| | A perception shared by a culture or group of people about key beliefs and issues such as death, God and the meaning of life that influences interaction with others. |

# CHAPTER 12
# RELATING TO FAMILY

## OBJECTIVES

After studying the material in this chapter of *Interpersonal Communication: Relating to Others* and completing the exercises in this section of the study guide, you should understand:

1. the definition of family and the difference between the natural, blended, single-parent, and extended families,
2. the four approaches to studying family communication--social-descriptive, communication skills and enrichment, therapeutic, and systems approaches,
3. the key principles of family systems theory,
4. the significance of the cohesion and adaptability model of family functioning, and
5. how to improve family relationships by using the communication characteristics of a healthy family.

## STUDY QUESTIONS

You should be able to answer the following questions:

1. What is a family?
2. How are the four types of families described?
3. What are the main elements of each of the four approaches to the study of family communication?
4. What are the key principles of the family communication system?
5. How does the Circumplex Model of Family Systems relate to communication in the family unit? Be able to define adaptability and cohesion.
6. How do role expectations affect family satisfaction?
7. What is the difference between institutional marriages and companionship marriages?
8. What are the differences between independent couples, traditional couples, and separates?
9. What are the communication characteristics of a healthy family?
10. What is documentation?

# EXERCISE 12.1    INVESTIGATING YOUR FAMILY RULES

**Purpose:**
1.    To help you understand the social-descriptive approach to studying family communication.
2.    To help you become aware of how your family rules, roles, patterns, traditions, and norms evolved.

**Directions:**
1.    Reflect back on the family in which you grew up.
2.    Answer the following questions about communication behavior by stating a rule your family had in regard to the question.

---

What topics could not be talked about openly?  ("Never discuss sex with Dad.")

How did your family handle conflict situations?  ("Do as I say, not as I do.")

Whom did you talk to about serious matters?  ("Mom listens better than Dad.")

Who talked to whom and when could they talk?  ("The boys talked to Mom and the girls talked to Dad.")

In what circumstances did subgroups or hierarchies appear to form in your family? ("When you want to get your way, go to Mom and Dad with at least one sibling.")

_____

_____

How comfortable were your family members with touching behavior? ("Don't go to bed without kissing Mom and Dad.")

_____

_____

How would you describe the communication patterns, in general, in your family--closed, open, sarcastic, friendly and warm, etc.? (Sarcastic humor covers hidden feelings.)

_____

_____

What language (words or phrases) was not accepted? (No profanity allowed.)

_____

_____

What rules did you have about eye contact? ("Look at me when I am talking to you!")

_____

_____

What rules were there regarding voice? ("No screaming in the house.")

_____

_____

What rules existed about clothing and appearance? ("Take off your shoes at the door.")

_____

_____

**Questions:**

1. Which of your rules do you still follow within your family?  Why?

2. Which rules have changed for you?  Why?

3. How did you become aware of each of the rules you mentioned?  Who made the rule?  Was the rule stated explicitly to you or did you learn it by experience?

4. Which rules will (did) you take with you into your own family?

# EXERCISE 12.2    UNDERSTANDING THE FAMILY AS A SYSTEM

## Purpose:
1.    To help you understand the family as a communication system.
2.    To investigate how your family is interdependent, complex, open, and adaptive.

## Directions:
1.    Observe your current family or your family of origin.
2.    Give an example for each of the aspects of the family system listed below.
3.    Explain the communication behavior your family used in each situation described.

---

## FAMILY SYSTEMS ARE INTERDEPENDENT

Describe a situation that happened in your family that affected every member of the family in some way.

_____

_____

_____

How did you communicate? _____

_____

## FAMILY SYSTEMS ARE COMPLEX

Discuss a time when members of your family had different meanings or interpretations of a single event.

_____

_____

_____

How did you communicate? _____

_____

# FAMILY SYSTEMS ARE OPEN

Discuss a time when something that happened outside the family had an impact or influence on the members of the family.

_____

_____

_____

How did you communicate? _____

_____


# FAMILY SYSTEMS ARE ADAPTIVE

Discuss a time when a change took place to which your family had to adjust.

_____

_____

_____

How did you communicate? _____

_____


## Questions:

1. What did you learn about your family by doing this exercise?


2. Which situations turned out well for your family? Not well?


3. How could you change your communication behaviors to deal with the situations in a more productive, cohesive way?

# EXERCISE 12.3    READJUSTING YOUR FAMILY

## Purpose:

1.    To identify the significant events in your life that have made an impact on your family interactions.
2.    To determine your family level of cohesion and adaptability following these events.

## Directions:

1.    Under "Number of Occurrences" indicate how many times in the past year each of the events has occurred.
2.    Multiply the number under "Scale Value" by the number of occurrences of each event and place the answer under "Your Score."
3.    Add the figures under "Your Score" to find your total for the past year.

### FAMILY READJUSTMENT SCALE

| Your Score | Scale Value | No. of Occurrences | Life Event |
|---|---|---|---|
| _____ | 100 | _____ | Death of spouse |
| _____ | 73 | _____ | Divorce |
| _____ | 65 | _____ | Marital Separation |
| _____ | 63 | _____ | Death of a close family member |
| _____ | 53 | _____ | Personal injury or illness |
| _____ | 50 | _____ | Marriage |
| _____ | 47 | _____ | Fired at work |
| _____ | 45 | _____ | Marital reconciliation |
| _____ | 45 | _____ | Retirement |
| _____ | 44 | _____ | Change in health of family member |
| _____ | 40 | _____ | Pregnancy |
| _____ | 39 | _____ | Sex difficulties |
| _____ | 39 | _____ | Gain of new family member |
| _____ | 39 | _____ | Business readjustment |
| _____ | 38 | _____ | Change in financial state |
| _____ | 37 | _____ | Death of a close friend |
| _____ | 36 | _____ | Change to different line of work |
| _____ | 35 | _____ | Change in number of arguments with spouse |
| _____ | 31 | _____ | Mortgage over $10,000 |
| _____ | 30 | _____ | Foreclosure of mortgage or loan |
| _____ | 29 | _____ | Change in responsibilities at work |
| _____ | 29 | _____ | Son or daughter leaving home |
| _____ | 29 | _____ | Trouble with in-laws |
| _____ | 28 | _____ | Outstanding personal achievement |
| _____ | 26 | _____ | Wife begins or stops work |

| | | | |
|---|---|---|---|
| _____ | 26 | _____ | Begin or end school |
| _____ | 25 | _____ | Change in living conditions |
| _____ | 24 | _____ | Revision of personal habits |
| _____ | 23 | _____ | Trouble with boss |
| _____ | 20 | _____ | Change in work hours or conditions |
| _____ | 20 | _____ | Change in residence |
| _____ | 20 | _____ | Change in schools |
| _____ | 19 | _____ | Change in recreation |
| _____ | 19 | _____ | Change in church activities |
| _____ | 18 | _____ | Change in social activities |
| _____ | 17 | _____ | Mortgage or loan less than $10,000 |
| _____ | 16 | _____ | Change in sleeping habits |
| _____ | 15 | _____ | Change in number of family get-togethers |
| _____ | 15 | _____ | Change in eating habits |
| _____ | 13 | _____ | Vacation |
| _____ | 12 | _____ | Christmas |
| _____ | 11 | _____ | Minor violations of the law |

_____ This is your total life change score for the past year.

If you scored at least 150 you have about a 50-50 chance of developing an illness or stress-induced health change. A score above 300 points increases the likelihood of a health change to almost 90 percent.

## Questions:

1. How did these event affect your family?
2. How did your family communicate about these events when they were occurring?
3. Where would you place your family on the adaptability continuum?

ADAPTABILITY

Rigid                                                       Chaotic

<---------------------------------------------------------------------------->

      Low                                              High

4. Where would you place your family on the cohesion continuum?

COHESION

Disengaged                                            Enmeshed

<---------------------------------------------------------------------------->

      Low                                              High

This exercise was reproduced for student use from the text, _Interpersonal Communication: Relating to Others._

## EXERCISE 12.4    IDENTIFYING ROLE EXPECTATIONS

**Purpose:**
1.    To help you to identify the role behavior expectations you take into your relationships.
2.    To determine whether your expectations are the same as or different than those of a significant person in your life.

**Directions:**
1.    Indicate which of the behaviors listed on the questionnaire below are the *primary* responsibility of the wife (W), the husband (H), or both (H/W).
2.    Beside each response, state the reasons you responded as you did.

_____    taking out the garbage

_____    writing thank-you notes

_____    initiating sexual activity

_____    balancing the check book

_____    changing diapers

_____    bringing home a paycheck

_____    disciplining the children

_____    doing the laundry

_____    planning for retirement

_____    cooking

_____    cleaning the bathrooms

_____    changing the oil in the car

_____    driving children to school

_____    mending clothes

_____    cleaning gutters on the house

_____    buying birthday presents for the parents

Ask your spouse, person you are dating, or friend to fill out this questionnaire:

**Directions:**
1.   Indicate which of the behaviors listed on the questionnaire below are the *primary* responsibility of the wife (W), the husband (H), or both (H/W).
2.   Beside each response, state the reasons you responded as you did.

_____ taking out the garbage

_____ writing thank-you notes

_____ initiating sexual activity

_____ balancing the check book

_____ changing diapers

_____ bringing home a paycheck

_____ disciplining the children

_____ doing the laundry

_____ planning for retirement

_____ cooking

_____ cleaning the bathrooms

_____ changing the oil in the car

_____ driving children to school

_____ mending clothes

_____ cleaning gutters on the house

_____ buying birthday presents for the parents

**Questions:**
1.   On which items did your partner agree with you?
2.   On which items did your partner disagree with you?
3.   If you were to live together, how would you handle the differences in your role expectations?

# EXERCISE 12.5    DEFINING ROLE IMAGES

## Purpose:
1.    To identify role behavior in your family.

## Directions:
1.    For each of the following images, name the person or persons in your current family or family of origin who plays the role. (Not all of the roles may be represented in every family.)

1.    The martyr--does most of the cooking, serving, and cleaning up.

_____

2.    The pet--the spoiled one who always gets the last spoonful of stuffing and the biggest slice of cake.

_____

3.    The victim--two hours late, but it's not his or her fault.  It never is!

_____

4.    The rebel--if everyone's dressed up, he or she wears old jeans, and then sits back and waits for the fireworks.

_____

5.    The peacemaker--he or she will make sure that everyone stays civil and then will be the one to suffer with heartburn.

_____

6.    The smart one--he or she hasn't seen the movie, but knows it's rotten.  You don't even argue.  Why invite the fight you know you'll lose?

_____

## Questions:
1.    How easy was it to identify the images you hold of your family members?
2.    Which roles were the hardest to match to a family member?  The easiest?
3.    What images are shared by all the members?
4.    In how many of the roles do you see yourself?  How do you feel about that?
5.    Do you think each member of your family would complete this questionnaire the same as you did?

(Adapted from Berko, et al. *Connecting*. Orlando, FL: Harcourt Brace)

## EXERCISE 12.6    ASSESSING YOUR FAMILY COMMUNICATION SKILLS

### Purpose:
1.    To become aware of how you communicate within your family unit.

### Directions:
1.    Think of your current family or your family of origin.
2.    Complete the following Family Communication Diagnostic Test to assess your communication skills.

### FAMILY COMMUNICATION DIAGNOSTIC TEST

|  |  | Usually | Sometimes | Seldom |
|---|---|---|---|---|
| 1. | Is it difficult for you to converse with other family members? | _____ | _____ | _____ |
| 2. | Do you feel other family members lack respect for you? | _____ | _____ | _____ |
| 3. | During family discussions, if it difficult for you to admit that you are wrong when you recognize that you are wrong about something? | _____ | _____ | _____ |
| 4. | Is it difficult to accept constructive criticism from other family members? | _____ | _____ | _____ |
| 5. | Do you pretend that you are listening to other family members when you are not really listening? | _____ | _____ | _____ |
| 6. | Do you find yourself being inattentive while in conversation with other family members? | _____ | _____ | _____ |
| 7. | Do you misunderstand other family members? | _____ | _____ | _____ |
| 8. | Are you dissatisfied with the way you settle your disagreements with members of your family? | _____ | _____ | _____ |

9.     Do you fail to express disagreement
with other family members because
you are afraid they will
get angry?        _____       _____       _____

10.    When a problem arises between
you and another family member,
do you become emotionally
upset?        _____       _____       _____

11.    Does it upset you a great deal
when another family member
disagrees with you?        _____       _____       _____

12.    Is it difficult to confide in other
family members?        _____       _____       _____

13.    Do you feel other family members
wish you were a different type of
person?        _____       _____       _____

14.    Do other family members fail to
understand your feelings?        _____       _____       _____

If you checked "usually" more than three times then your family communication skills
clearly need sharpening.

This exercise was reproduced for student use from the text, *Interpersonal
Communication: Relating to Others.*

# EXERCISE 12.7    WATCHING FAMILIES COMMUNICATE

## Purpose:
1.    To observe communication patterns in different families.
2.    To become aware of healthy and unhealthy communication behaviors in families.

## Directions:
1.    Choose two television sit-coms that revolve around a family.  Choose different family types or different cultural families.  The programs may be current or reruns.  Some examples are: *Cosby Show, Full House, Roseanne, Married with Children, Hangin' With Mr. Cooper, Coach, Fresh Prince of Bel-Air, The Nanny, Home Improvement, Party of Five, Family Matters.*
2.    Describe the family type.
3.    Find examples of the communication-related behaviors that illustrate healthy and unhealthy families.

**TV SHOW #1:**    Name: _____

Describe the type of family: _____

_____

## Communication Patterns

1.    Take time to talk about relationships and feelings. _____

_____

_____

2.    Listen and clarify the meaning of messages. _____

_____

_____

3.    Support and encourage one another. _____

_____

_____

4.  Use productive strategies for managing conflict, stress, and change. _____

_____

_____

**TV SHOW #2:**     Name: _____

Describe the type of family. _____

_____

## Communication Patterns

1.  Talking about relationships and feelings. _____

_____

_____

2.  Listening and clarifying the meaning of messages. _____

_____

_____

3.  Support and encouragement for one another. _____

_____

_____

4.  Strategies for managing conflict, stress, and change. _____

_____

_____

## Questions:
1.  How were your selected television shows similar in communication patterns? How were they different?
2.  What dysfunctional communication behaviors did you observe most often?
3.  What healthy communication behaviors were used most frequently?

| | |
|---|---|
| Family | Natural Family |
| Blended Family | Single-Parent Family |
| Extended Family | Family of Origin |
| Social-Descriptive Approach | Communication Skills and Enrichment Approach |
| Therapeutic Approach | Systems Approach |
| Circumplex Model of Family Interaction | Family Adaptability |

| | |
|---|---|
| A mother, father and their biological children. | A unit made up of any number of persons who live in relationship with one another over time in a common living space who are usually, but not always, united by marriage and kinship. |
| One parent raising one or more children. | Two adults and their children. Because of divorce, separation, death or adoption, the children may be the product of other parents, or of just one of the adults who is raising them. |
| The family in which you were raised. | Relatives such as aunts, uncles, cousins or grandparents who are part of the family unit. |
| An approach to studying family communication which focuses on the prescriptive principles and skills that are designed to help even well-functioning families improve their communication skills. | An approach to studying family communication by investigating the rules, roles, patterns, traditions, and norms of family life. |
| A holistic approach that views a family as an interdependent system of related individuals. | An approach to studying family communication that tries to help dysfunctional families identify and manage problematic communication issues. |
| Refers to a family member's ability to modify and respond to changes in the family's power structure and roles. | A model which shows the relationships between family adaptability, cohesion, and communication. |

| | |
|---|---|
| Family Cohesion | Family Communication |
| Role Expectation | Institutional Marriage |
| Companionship Marriage | Independent Couples |
| Traditional Couples | Separate Couples |
| Documentation | |

| | |
|---|---|
| The way in which family members mutually influence each other. | Refers to the emotional bonding and feelings of togetherness that families experience. |
| A marriage in which partners assume traditional husband and wife roles. | The consistent way we expect someone to behave. |
| A marriage relationship in which the couples accept change and uncertainty, have high role flexibility and may assume less conventional gender roles. | A marriage in which partners have flexible roles. |
| A marriage relationship in which the husband and wife maintain more physical and psychological distance between themselves and their partner. | A marriage relationship in which the husband and wife operate with a well-defined interdependent relationship. |
| | A listening technique in which you state what behavior led to your understanding or interpretation of your partner's behavior. |

# CHAPTER 13
# RELATING TO FRIENDS AND LOVERS

## OBJECTIVES

After studying the material in this chapter of *Interpersonal Communication: Relating to Others* and completing the exercises in this section of the study guide, you should understand:

1.    the reasons for friendships and what the functions are,
2.    the difference between rules for establishing and rules for maintaining friendships,
3.    the difference between acquaintances, casual friends, and close friends,
4.    the characteristics of childhood, adolescent, adult friendships, and friendships of the elderly,
5.    how the strategies of using friendship opportunities, encouraging others, understanding the process of development, and using communication skills help maintain friendships,
6.    the behaviors that result in losing friends,
7.    the difference between love and friendship, and
8.    the difference between the six different types of love.

## STUDY QUESTIONS

You should be able to answer the following questions:

1.    What are the functions of friendship?
2.    What motivates us to develop friendships?
3.    What functions do friendships perform for us?
4.    What are the rules for establishing friendships?
5.    What are the rules for maintaining friendships?
6.    Explain the difference between an acquaintance, a casual friend, and a close friend?
7.    What are the stages of childhood friendships?
8.    How do adolescent friendships differ from adult friendships?
9.    What are the communication strategies you can use to make friends?
10.   What behaviors contribute to losing friends?
11.   How is love different from friendship?
12.   Explain each of the six types of love.

**EXERCISE 13.1    CHOOSING YOUR FRIENDS**

<u>**Purpose:**</u>
1.    To help you become aware of why you have friendships
2.    To understand the reasons you chose some people for close friends and others for casual friends.

<u>**Directions:**</u>
1.    Think of your best friend and fill out the questionnaire below.
2.    Think of a casual friend and repeat the questionnaire.


My best friend is _____.


How did we meet? _____

_____

_____


Why did we become friends? _____

_____

_____


How does my friend meet my needs? _____

_____

_____


How do I meet the needs of my friend? _____

_____

_____

A casual friend of mine is _____.

How did we meet? _____

_____

_____

Why did we become friends? _____

_____

_____

How does my friend meet my needs? _____

_____

_____

How do I meet the needs of my friend? _____

_____

_____

## **Questions:**

1.  What are the similarities or differences between the way you met each of your friends?

2.  What are the differences between the reasons you became friends?

3.  What are the differences between your needs that each of the friends meets?

4.  What are the differences between the needs you meet for each of the friends?

5.  How does your communication behavior change between your best friend and your casual friend--what you talk about, how much information you share, etc.?

# EXERCISE 13.2   ADVERTISING FOR FRIENDSHIPS

## Purpose:
1.    To understand characteristics you look for in different types of friendships.

## Directions:
1.    Write ads for people to fill the following friendship vacancies in your life:
    a.    a male with whom you want to have a casual friendship
    b.    a female with whom you want to have a casual friendship
    c.    a person with whom you want to have a loving and caring friendship
    d.    a person from another (name a specific country) culture with whom you want to have a friendship
    e.    a person with whom you want to have a work friendship
2.    In each ad, identify the personal characteristics and communication behaviors you want in the other person.
3.    Identify the personal characteristics and communication behaviors you have to offer to the other person.


## ADVERTISEMENT FOR A CASUAL MALE FRIEND

_____

_____

_____

_____

_____


## ADVERTISEMENT FOR A CASUAL FEMALE FRIEND

_____

_____

_____

_____

_____

# ADVERTISEMENT FOR A CARING AND LOVING FRIEND

_____

_____

_____

_____

_____

# ADVERTISEMENT FOR A FRIEND FROM ANOTHER CULTURE

_____

_____

_____

_____

_____

# ADVERTISEMENT FOR A FRIEND FROM WORK

_____

_____

_____

_____

_____

## Questions:

1. How do the personal characteristics differ in your ads?  Stay the same?  Why?
2. How do the communication behaviors differ?  Stay the same?  Why?
3. What specific goals would you have for each type of friendship--escape loneliness, share experiences, give emotional support, talk, etc.?

## EXERCISE 13.3     ESTABLISHING RULES FOR FRIENDSHIPS

### Purpose:
1.     To identify the rules you have for friendships.
2.     To understand that other people define friendship differently than you do.

### Directions:
1.     Make a list of the rules you have for your friendships--if you say you will do something, do it;  give each other time with other friends, etc.
2.     Ask three other people (acquaintances, preferably) to make lists of the rules they have for friendships.
3.     Compare the lists.


## RULES I HAVE FOR FRIENDSHIPS

1.     _____

2.     _____

3.     _____

4.     _____

5.     _____


## RULES OTHERS HAVE FOR FRIENDSHIPS -- PERSON #1

1.     _____

2.     _____

3.     _____

4.     _____

5.     _____

## RULES OTHERS HAVE FOR FRIENDSHIPS -- PERSON #2

1. _____

2. _____

3. _____

4. _____

5. _____


## RULES OTHERS HAVE FOR FRIENDSHIPS -- PERSON #3

1. _____

2. _____

3. _____

4. _____

5. _____


## Questions:

1. How are your rules the same as the others' rules?  How are they different?


2. With which other person (people) would you want to establish a friendship?


3. With which other person (people) would you not want to establish a friendship?

# EXERCISE 13.4   REMEMBERING FRIENDS

## Purpose:
1.    To understand why some friendships last and others do not last.

## Directions:
1.    Make lists of the friends you had in childhood, during adolescence, and those you have currently.
2.    State why each person was (is) your friend.

**My Childhood Friends**                    **Why Friendship Existed**

_____                    _____
_____                    _____
_____                    _____
_____                    _____
_____                    _____

**My Adolescent Friends**

_____                    _____
_____                    _____
_____                    _____
_____                    _____
_____                    _____

**My Friends Today**

_____                    _____
_____                    _____
_____                    _____
_____                    _____
_____                    _____

## Questions:

1.    Are any friends in all three columns?  Why or why not?


2.    How did the reasons for your friendships change or stay the same?

# EXERCISE 13.5     CHOOSING FRIENDS FOR SPECIFIC SITUATIONS

**Purpose:**

1.      To help you become aware of who your friends are in specific situations.

**Directions:**

1.      Complete the friendship inventory below, identifying the friends you turn to for support or to celebrate a major event.

---

1.      You have an extra ticket to a concert or major sports event.  List the three people you would call, in order of preference.

     1..    _____

     2.    _____

     3.    _____

2.      You have just learned of the unexpected death of a family member.  Who would you call first?  Second?  Third?

     1.    _____

     2.    _____

     3.    _____

3.      You are going on a cruise and have learned that you can bring a friend along for free.  List in order of preference the first three people you would invite to go.

     1.    _____

     2.    _____

     3.    _____

4.      As you are driving through a small town, you get a traffic ticket and you don't have your car registration or driver's license with you.  You are taken to jail.  List in order the first three people you would call.

     1.    _____

     2.    _____

     3.    _____

## EXERCISE 13.6    LOSING FRIENDS

**Purpose:**
1.    To help you become aware of the reasons you have lost some friends.

**Directions:**
1.    Identify four of your past friendships that are have ended.
2.    List the reasons that each of the friendships ended.

## FRIENDSHIP #1

Describe the friendship:

_____

_____

State the reasons the friendship ended:

_____

_____

_____

## FRIENDSHIP #2

Describe the friendship:

_____

_____

State the reasons the friendship ended:

_____

_____

# FRIENDSHIP #3

Describe the friendship:

_____

_____

State the reasons the friendship ended:

_____

_____

_____

# FRIENDSHIP #4

Describe the friendship:

_____

_____

State the reasons the friendship ended:

_____

_____

_____

## Questions:

1. Which reasons for ending the friendships were the same?

2. Which reasons for ending the friendships were different?

3. What did you learn about your attitude about friendships?

4. What could have been done to preserve each of the friendships?

## EXERCISE 13.7    COMMUNICATING WITH FRIENDS

**Purpose:**
1.    To become aware of your communication behavior patterns in attending, active listening, and empathy..
2.    To understand how you communicate with friends

**Directions:**
1.    Complete the following communication behavior inventory.
2.    Answer each question in terms of how you interact with your friends.
3.    Answer each question honestly.
4.    Answer the questions as quickly as possible according to your immediate response.  Do not change your answers once you record them.
5.    Do not consult with anyone while you are answering the questions.
6.    Use the following scale to respond to the questions:

| | | |
|---|---|---|
| 1 | = | Rarely or Never |
| 2 | = | Sometimes |
| 3 | = | Most often |

### SELF-INVENTORY OF COMMUNICATION BEHAVIOR

| | Most often | Sometimes | Rarely |
|---|---|---|---|
| 1.    Do you find it difficult to look directly at a friend who is speaking to you? | _____ | _____ | _____ |
| 2.    When a friend is speaking to you, do you face the person squarely? | _____ | _____ | _____ |
| 3.    When a friend is speaking to you, do you doodle or play with some object? | _____ | _____ | _____ |
| 4.    When a friend is speaking to you, do you get the feeling he/she is not sure whether you heard them or not? | _____ | _____ | _____ |
| 5.    Are you aware of your facial expressions when a friend is speaking to you? | _____ | _____ | _____ |
| 6.    Do you observe the body posture of the friend who is speaking to you? | _____ | _____ | _____ |
| 7.    When a friend is speaking to you, do you find it difficult to focus on what he/she is saying? | _____ | _____ | _____ |

8. When a friend is speaking to you, do you listen to how he/she sounds? _____ _____ _____

9. Do you remain silent until your friend speaking has finished? _____ _____ _____

10. Do you observe the facial expressions of the friend who is speaking to you? _____ _____ _____

11. When a friend is speaking to you, do you try to put yourself in his/her place? _____ _____ _____

12. Do you pretend to be listening to your friend when you aren't? _____ _____ _____

13. When a friend is speaking to you, do you let him/her just assume you know what he/she has said? _____ _____ _____

14. Do you try to identify the feelings being conveyed by a friend who is speaking to you? _____ _____ _____

15. When a friend is speaking to you, do you say you understand even if you don't? _____ _____ _____

TOTAL SCORE _____ _____ _____

**Explanation of scoring:**

Questions 1-5 reflect your ability to pay attention to your friends when they are speaking.
Questions 6-10 reflect your ability to actively listen to your friends when they are speaking.
Questions 11-15 reflect your ability to have empathy with your friends when they are speaking to you.
Record your scores for each set of questions:

**Attending**          **Active listening**          **Empathy**

_____          _____          _____

A score of 5 or below indicates you need to work on this communication behavior.
A score of 11 or above indicates the you communicate effectively in this area.

**EXERCISE 13.8    LOVING, LIKING, AND FEELING**

**Purpose:**
1.    To determine the amount of liking or loving you feel for another person.
2.    To determine the compatibility of feelings between you and another person.

**Directions:**
1.    Fill out the questionnaire below.
2.    **Optional:** Ask a friend, dating partner, lover or spouse to fill out the second questionnaire.

## LIKING AND LOVING

Insert the name of a friend, dating partner, lover or spouse in each of the following statements.  Give each statement a rating according to the following scale:

|   |   |   |
|---|---|---|
| 1 | = | Disagree completely |
| 5 | = | Agree to some extent |
| 9 | = | Agree completely |

_____    1.    I feel responsible for _____'s well-being.
_____    2.    If I could never be with _____ I would feel miserable.
_____    3.    I have great confidence in _____ 's good judgment.
_____    4.    I feel I can confide in _____ about virtually anything.
_____    5.    If I were lonely, my first thought would be to seek out _____.
_____    6.    I think _____ is one of those people who quickly win respect.
_____    7.    I think that _____ is unusually well-adjusted.
_____    8.    _____ is the sort of person who I would like to be.
_____    9.    I would do almost anything for _____.
_____    10.    In my opinion _____ is an exceptionally mature person.
_____    11.    It would be hard for me to get along without _____.
_____    12.    _____ is one of the most likable people I know.
_____    13.    I would forgive _____ for practically anything.
_____    14.    Most people would react favorably to _____ after a brief acquaintance.
_____    15.    I would highly recommend _____ for a responsible job.
_____    16.    One of my primary concerns is _____'s welfare.
_____    17.    It seems to me that it is very easy for _____ to gain admiration.
_____    18.    I would greatly enjoy being confided in by _____.

Scoring:
     Add the scores for statements 3, 6, 7, 8, 10, 12, 14, 15, and 17.  This is the amount of liking you have for the other person.  The higher the "liking" score the greater likelihood that this person is more a friend than a lover.
     Add the scores for statements 1, 2, 4, 5, 9, 11, 13, 16 and 18.  This indicated the amount of loving you feel for the other person.

# LIKING AND LOVING

Insert the name of the person who gave you this questionnaire in each of the following statements.

Give each statement a rating according to the following scale:

| | | |
|---|---|---|
| 1 | = | Disagree completely |
| 5 | = | Agree to some extent |
| 9 | = | Agree completely |

_____ 1. I feel responsible for _____'s well-being.

_____ 2. If I could never be with _____ I would feel miserable.

_____ 3. I have great confidence in _____ 's good judgment.

_____ 4. I feel I can confide in _____ about virtually anything.

_____ 5. If I were lonely, my first thought would be to seek out _____.

_____ 6. I think _____ is one of those people who quickly win respect.

_____ 7. I think that _____ is unusually well-adjusted.

_____ 8. _____ is the sort of person who I would like to be.

_____ 9. I would do almost anything for _____.

_____ 10. In my opinion _____ is an exceptionally mature person.

_____ 11. It would be hard for me to get along without _____.

_____ 12. _____ is one of the most likable people I know.

_____ 13. I would forgive _____ for practically anything.

_____ 14. Most people would react favorably to _____ after a brief acquaintance.

_____ 15. I would highly recommend _____ for a responsible job.

_____ 16. One of my primary concerns is _____'s welfare.

_____ 17. It seems to me that it is very easy for _____ to gain admiration.

_____ 18. I would greatly enjoy being confided in by _____.

Scoring:

Add the scores for statements 3, 6, 7, 8, 10, 12, 14, 15, and 17. This is the amount of liking you have for the other person. The higher the "liking" score the greater likelihood that this person is more a friend than a lover.

Add the scores for statements 1, 2, 4, 5, 9, 11, 13, 16 and 18. This indicated the amount of loving you feel for the other person.

(Reproduced for student use from *Interpersonal Communication: Relating to Others.*)

## EXERCISE 13.9    DISCOVERING YOUR OWN LOVE PROFILE

**Purpose:**

1.    To become aware of your attitude toward "love."

**Directions:**

Rate each of the following statements on a 1-5 scale:

|  |  |  |
|---|---|---|
| 1 | = | Strongly disagree |
| 2 | = | Disagree |
| 3 | = | Neutral |
| 4 | = | Agree |
| 5 | = | Strongly agree |

_____ 1.    You cannot love unless you have first had a caring relationship for a while.

_____ 2.    The best kind of love grows out of a long friendship.

_____ 3.    Kissing, cuddling, and sex should not be rushed into; they will happen naturally when intimacy has grown.

_____ 4.    Love is really deep friendship, not a mysterious, mystical emotion.

_____ 5.    I believe that "love at first sight" is possible.

_____ 6.    We kissed each other soon after we met because we both wanted to.

_____ 7.    Usually the first thing that attracts my attention to a person is a pleasing appearance.

_____ 8.    Strong physical attraction is one of the best things about being in love.

_____ 9.    When things are not going right with us, my stomach gets upset.

_____ 10.    Once when I thought a love affair was over, I saw him or her again and the old feelings came surging back.

_____ 11.    If my partner ignores me for a while, I sometimes do really stupid things to try to get his or her attention.

_____ 12.    When my partner does not pay attention to me, I feel sick all over.

_____ 13.    I try to use my own strength to help my partner through difficult times, even when he or she is behaving foolishly.

_____ 14. I am usually willing to sacrifice my own wishes in favor of my partner's.

_____ 15. If my partner had a baby by someone else, I would want to raise it and care for it as if it were my own.

_____ 16. I would rather break up with my partner than stand in his or her way.

_____ 17. For practical reasons, I would consider what he or she is going to become before I commit myself.

_____ 18. You should plan your life before choosing a partner.

_____ 19. A main consideration is choosing a partner is how he or she reflects on my family.

_____ 20. I would not date anyone that I would not want to fall in love with.

_____ 21. At least once I had to plan carefully to keep two of my lovers from finding out about each other.

_____ 22. I can get over love affairs pretty easily and quickly.

_____ 23. My partner would get upset if he or she knew some of the things I have done with other people.

_____ 24. What he or she does not know about me will not hurt my partner.

## Scoring:

Add your scores for statements 1-4. Divide by 4. This is your score for the friendship factor (storge).

Add your scores for statements 5-8 and divide by 4. This is your score for the passionate factor (eros).

Add your scores for statements 9-12; divide by 4. This is your score for the possessive factor (mania).

Add your scores for statements 13-16; divide by 4. This is your score for the selflessness factor (agape).

Add your scores for statements 17-20; divide by 4. This is your score for the practical factor (pragma).

Add your scores for statements 21-14; divide by 4. This is your score for the game-playing factor (ludis).

See the text, _Interpersonal Communication: Relating to Others,_ for the averages for each type of love.

## EXERCISE 13.10    WATCHING FRIENDSHIPS

**Purpose:**

1. To identify the communication behaviors used with acquaintances, casual friends, and close friends.
2. To identify the communication behaviors that are the most important in maintaining friendships.

**Directions:**

1. Watch a television program or series of programs that show the interaction of friends. Examples to watch are *Friends, Coach, Wings, Hope & Gloria, Seinfeld.*
2. Observe the communication skills that are used between the friends on the show.
3. Identify the ability of the characters to listen, respond, empathize, be open, adaptive and sensitive to each other.
4. Determine how the behaviors affected the friendships.

Describe the program and the characters involved.

_____

_____

Describe the listening behavior.

_____

_____

Effect on the friendships.

_____

_____

Describe the confirming and disconfirming responses.

_____

_____

Effect on the friendships.

_____

_____

Describe the amount of empathy.

_____

_____

Effect on the friendships.

_____

_____

Describe the openness, especially self-disclosure.

_____

_____

Effect on the friendships.

_____

_____

Describe the adaptability and sensitivity to each other.

_____

_____

Effect on the friendships.

_____

_____

## Questions:

1. What behaviors made a positive impact on the friendships?
2. What behaviors made a negative impact on the friendships?
3. Were there any differences between gender in the way communication behaviors were used?
4. What intercultural differences, if any, did you observe in the way the characters communicated?

| | |
|---|---|
| Need for Inclusion | Need for Control |
| Need for affection | Intimacy |
| Eros Love | Ludis Love |
| Storge Love | Mania Love |
| Pragma Love | Agape Love |

| | |
|---|---|
| The interpersonal need for some degree of dominion in our relationships as well as the need to be controlled. | The need to be included and to include others in group activities. |
| The degree of closeness we feel with another person. | The need to give and receive love, support, warmth and intimacy. |
| Playful, game playing love based upon the enjoyment of others. | Sexual, erotic love based upon the pursuit of physical beauty and pleasure. |
| Obsessive love driven by mutual needs. | Solid love of friendship based upon trust and caring. |
| Selfless love based upon giving of oneself for others. | Practical love based upon mutual benefits. |

# CHAPTER 14
# RELATING TO COLLEAGUES

## OBJECTIVES

After studying the material in this chapter of *Interpersonal Communication: Relating to Others* and completing the exercises in this section of the study guide, you should understand:

1. the difference between upward, downward, horizontal, and outward communication,
2. the difference between the five different leadership styles,
3. how communication skills enhance your ability to lead and follow,
4. how to use the four strategies for effectively interviewing for a job,
5. how to use the three strategies for interviewing others for a job,
6. how to give and receive feedback during a performance review,
7. the eight characteristics of an effective team,
8. how to use skills, tools, and the steps for problem solving in teams, and
9. the role and effects of technology on interpersonal relationships in the workplace.

## STUDY QUESTIONS

You should be able to answer the following questions:

1. What is the difference between upward, downward, horizontal, and outward communication in organizations?
2. What are the types of sexual harassment?
3. What is the difference between a task-oriented and a relationship-oriented leader?
4. What is the difference between the four leadership styles?
5. How can you enhance your leadership skills?
6. What are the task functions and the relationship functions of effective leaders? How can you improve your followership skills?
7. What is the definition of an interview?
8. What can you do to prepare for a job interview?
9. How do you interview someone to fill a job position?
10. What is the difference between an open question, a closed question, and probing questions?
11. What is a performance review?
12. What can you do when receiving a performance review?
13. What do employers do when giving an effective performance review?
14. What are the characteristics of an effective team?

15. What communication skills are needed to develop effective problem solving in teams?
16. What is the role of technology in the workplace?
17. How does technology affect communication in organizations?

# EXERCISE 14.1     RECOGNIZING MESSAGE DIRECTION

## Purpose:
1.     To identify examples of upward, downward, horizontal, and outward communication in your workplaces. (Don't forget that school and home can be considered workplaces for this exercise.)

## Directions:
1.     Find two examples of each type of message over the next few days.
2.     Identify the relationship between the sender and the receiver.

---

## UPWARD MESSAGES

| Sender | Receiver | Content of message |
|--------|----------|--------------------|
|        |          |                    |
|        |          |                    |

## DOWNWARD MESSAGES

| Sender | Receiver | Content of message |
|--------|----------|--------------------|
|        |          |                    |
|        |          |                    |

## HORIZONTAL MESSAGES

| Sender | Receiver | Content of message |
|--------|----------|--------------------|
|        |          |                    |
|        |          |                    |

## OUTWARD MESSAGES

| Sender | Receiver | Content of message |
|--------|----------|--------------------|
|        |          |                    |
|        |          |                    |

## Questions:

1.  How did the messages affect the relationships between the senders and the receivers?

_____

_____

# EXERCISE 14.2    IDENTIFYING WORKPLACE WANTS

## Purpose:
1.    To help you identify what is important to you in the work environment.
2.    To help you understand that people have different perceptions of what is important in the work environment.

## Directions:
1.    Rank each of the following work-related items according to their importance.
2.    Project how you think your partner would rank each item.
3.    Have a person with whom you work rank the items according to the importance to him or her and to project how he or she thinks you would rank each item.
4.    Discuss your answers with each other when you have completed the questionnaire.

Use the following scale to rank the items:

| Not Important | | | | Very Important |
|---|---|---|---|---|
| 1 | 2 | 3 | 4 | 5 |

| | | My personal ranking | My partner's ranking of me |
|---|---|---|---|
| 1. | Sensitivity to personal problems | _____ | _____ |
| 2. | Interesting work | _____ | _____ |
| 3. | Salary | _____ | _____ |
| 4. | Job security | _____ | _____ |
| 5. | Loyalty of company to employees | _____ | _____ |
| 6. | Tactful and constructive criticism | _____ | _____ |
| 7. | Appreciation for work | _____ | _____ |
| 8. | A sense of belonging | _____ | _____ |
| 9. | Good working conditions | _____ | _____ |
| 10. | Opportunities for advancement | _____ | _____ |
| | | My personal ranking | My partner's ranking of me |
| 1. | Sensitivity to personal problems | _____ | _____ |
| 2. | Interesting work | _____ | _____ |
| 3. | Salary | _____ | _____ |
| 4. | Job security | _____ | _____ |
| 5. | Loyalty of company to employees | _____ | _____ |
| 6. | Tactful and constructive criticism | _____ | _____ |
| 7. | Appreciation for work | _____ | _____ |
| 8. | A sense of belonging | _____ | _____ |
| 9. | Good working conditions | _____ | _____ |
| 10. | Opportunities for advancement | _____ | _____ |

Give this form to your partner.

Use the following scale to rank the items:

Not Important                                          Very Important
        1             2             3             4             5

|  |  | My personal ranking | My partner's ranking of me |
|---|---|---|---|
| 1. | Sensitivity to personal problems | _____ | _____ |
| 2. | Interesting work | _____ | _____ |
| 3. | Salary | _____ | _____ |
| 4. | Job security | _____ | _____ |
| 5. | Loyalty of company to employees | _____ | _____ |
| 6. | Tactful and constructive criticism | _____ | _____ |
| 7. | Appreciation for work | _____ | _____ |
| 8. | A sense of belonging | _____ | _____ |
| 9. | Good working conditions | _____ | _____ |
| 10. | Opportunities for advancement | _____ | _____ |

|  |  | My personal ranking | My partner's ranking of me |
|---|---|---|---|
| 1. | Sensitivity to personal problems | _____ | _____ |
| 2. | Interesting work | _____ | _____ |
| 3. | Salary | _____ | _____ |
| 4. | Job security | _____ | _____ |
| 5. | Loyalty of company to employees | _____ | _____ |
| 6. | Tactful and constructive criticism | _____ | _____ |
| 7. | Appreciation for work | _____ | _____ |
| 8. | A sense of belonging | _____ | _____ |
| 9. | Good working conditions | _____ | _____ |
| 10. | Opportunities for advancement | _____ | _____ |

(Taken from Shockley-Zalabak, P. (1991) *Fundamentals of Organizational Communication*. White Plains, NY: Longman.)

# EXERCISE 14.3     LEADING LESSONS

**Purpose:**

1.     To help you identify your perception of trait qualities of leadership.

**Directions:**

1.     Think of your experiences with leadership and leaders.
2.     Fill out the following questionnaire that focuses on the idea that leadership
       qualities are within a person.

---

### Leadership Experiences

The following twenty-one statements have been used to describe leadership and leaders.
For each of the four incomplete sentences below, select from among the following
twenty-one statements the five that best reflect your experiences with leadership and
leaders. Statements may be used to complete more than one incomplete sentence.
(Taken from Shockley-Zalabak, P. (1991) *Fundamentals of Organizational
Communication*. White Plains, NY: Longman.)

*Statements Describing Leaders and Leadership*

1.     Leaders are born.
2.     Leadership ability can be developed.
3.     Leaders are high in intelligence.
4.     Leaders take initiative.
5.     Leaders deviate from norms.
6.     Leaders have good communication skills.
7.     Leaders are in the right place at the right time.
8.     Leaders are democratic.
9.     Leaders are autocratic.
10.    Leaders are risk takers.
11.    Leaders take a "hands off" approach.
12.    Leadership is situation specific.
13.    Leaders block ideas and punish opposition.
14.    Leaders seek ideas and encourage disagreement.
15.    Leaders ignore conflict.
16.    Leaders solicit feedback.
17.    Leaders are outcome oriented.
18.    Leaders share praise.
19.    Leaders set goals.
20.    Leaders blame those who fail.
21.    Leaders control their followers.

---

My experience with leadership and leaders has taught me that effective . . .

    1.

    2.

    3.

    4.

    5.

My experience with leadership and leaders has taught me that ineffective . . .

    1.

    2.

    3.

    4.

    5.

My experience with leadership and leaders has taught me that the most important aspects of leadership are . . .

    1.

    2.

    3.

    4.

    5.

My experience with leadership and leaders has taught me that the least important aspects of leadership are . . .

    1.

    2.

    3.

    4.

    5.

# EXERCISE 14.4    IDENTIFYING EFFECTIVE LEADERS

**Purpose**:
1.    To help you identify effective and ineffective leadership behaviors.

**Directions**:
1.    Identify 5 effective leaders by name--past or current.
2.    Describe the behaviors of the effective leaders.
3.    Identify 5 ineffective leaders by name.
4.    Describe the behaviors of those you think were ineffective leaders.

| EFFECTIVE LEADERS | BEHAVIORS |
|---|---|
|  |  |
|  |  |
|  |  |
|  |  |
|  |  |

| INEFFECTIVE LEADERS | BEHAVIORS |
|---|---|
| | |
| | |
| | |
| | |
| | |

## Questions:

1.   In what ways are the leaders on your list similar?

_____

_____

2.   In what ways are the leaders different?

_____

_____

# EXERCISE 14.5    ASSESSING YOUR LEADERSHIP STYLE

## Purpose:
1.    To help you determine your preferred style of leadership.

## Directions:
1.    Fill out the following questionnaire, focusing on your leadership behavior in a work group.

### Task-Person Leadership Questionnaire

The following items describe aspects of leadership behavior. Respond to each item according to the way you would be most likely to act if you were the leader of a work group. Circle whether you would be likely to behave in the described way always (A), frequently (F), occasionally (O), seldom (S), or never (N).

If I were the leader of a work group:

| | | | | | | |
|---|---|---|---|---|---|---|
| A | F | O | S | N | 1. | I would most likely act as the spokesman of the group. |
| A | F | O | S | N | 2. | I would encourage overtime work. |
| A | F | O | S | N | 3. | I would allow members complete freedom in their work. |
| A | F | O | S | N | 4. | I would encourage the use of uniform procedures. |
| A | F | O | S | N | 5. | I would permit the members to use their own judgment in problems. |
| A | F | O | S | N | 6. | I would stress the need to be ahead of competing groups. |
| A | F | O | S | N | 7. | I would speak as a representative of the group. |
| A | F | O | S | N | 8. | I would needle members to achieve greater effort. |
| A | F | O | S | N | 9. | I would try out my ideas in the group. |
| A | F | O | S | N | 10. | I would let the members do their work the way they think best. |
| A | F | O | S | N | 11. | I would work hard for a promotion. |
| A | F | O | S | N | 12. | I would be able to tolerate postponement and uncertainty. |
| A | F | O | S | N | 13. | I would speak for the group when visitors were present. |
| A | F | O | S | N | 14. | I would keep the work moving at a rapid pace. |
| A | F | O | S | N | 15. | I would turn members loose on a job and let them go to it. |
| A | F | O | S | N | 16. | I would settle conflicts when they occur in the group. |
| A | F | O | S | N | 17. | I would get swamped by details. |
| A | F | O | S | N | 18. | I would represent the group at outside meetings. |
| A | F | O | S | N | 19. | I would be reluctant to allow members any freedom of action. |
| A | F | O | S | N | 20. | I would decide what should be done and how it would be done. |
| A | F | O | S | N | 21. | I would push for increased production. |

| | | | | | | |
|---|---|---|---|---|---|---|
| A | F | O | S | N | 22. | I would let some members have authority which I should keep. |
| A | F | O | S | N | 23. | Things would usually turn out as I predict. |
| A | F | O | S | N | 24. | I would allow the group a high degree of initiative. |
| A | F | O | S | N | 25. | I would assign group members to particular tasks. |
| A | F | O | S | N | 26. | I would be willing to make changes. |
| A | F | O | S | N | 27. | I would ask the members to work harder. |
| A | F | O | S | N | 28. | I would trust group members to exercise good judgment. |
| A | F | O | S | N | 29. | I would schedule the work to be done. |
| A | F | O | S | N | 30. | I would refuse to explain my actions. |
| A | F | O | S | N | 31. | I would persuade others that my ideas are to their advantage. |
| A | F | O | S | N | 32. | I would permit the group to set its own pace. |
| A | F | O | S | N | 33. | I would urge the group to beat its previous record. |
| A | F | O | S | N | 34. | I would act without consulting the group. |
| A | F | O | S | N | 35. | I would ask that group members follow standard rules and regulations. |

## Scoring Procedures for Leadership:

1.  Circle the item number for questionnaire items 1, 4, 7, 13, 17, 18, 19, 20, 23, 29, 30, 31, 34, and 35.

2.  Write a 1 in front of the *circled items* to which you responded S (seldom) or N (never).

3.  Write a 1 in front of *items not circled* to which you responded A (always) or F(frequently).

4.  Circle the 1s which you have written in front of the following items: 3, 5, 8, 10, 12, 15, 17, 19, 22, 24, 26, 28, 30, 32, and 34.

5.  Count the circled 1s. This is your person orientation (P) score. Record the score in the blank following the letter P below.

6.  Count the uncircled 1s. This is your task orientation (T) score. Record this number in the blank following the letter T.

P _____     T _____

## Leadership Grid

In order to locate your position on the Leadership Grid below, find your score on the Person dimension (P), the horizontal axis of the graph. Next, move up the column corresponding to your P score to the cell that corresponds to your Task or T score. Place an X in the cell that represents your two scores.

| Task Score (T) | | | |
|---|---|---|---|
| 20 19 18 17 16 15 14 | Autocratic | | Democratic |
| 13 12 11 10 9 8 | | Situational | |
| 7 6 5 4 3 2 1 | Laissez-faire | | Relationship-oriented |

1  2  3  4  5  6  7  8  9  10  11  12  13  14  15

Person Orientation Score (P)

(Adapted from Blake, R. and Mouton, J. (1964) *The Managerial Grid.* Houston, TX: Gulf.)

**EXERCISE 14.6    PLANNING FOR AN INTERVIEW**

<u>**Purpose**</u>:
1.    To help you identify the skills and personality traits that might help you prepare for the unexpected questions which may be brought up in an interview.

<u>**Directions**</u>:
1.    Answer the following questions.

---

1.    List the special skills, interests, volunteer jobs, leadership/coaching activities you have.

2.    Identify and list four important achievements and the skills used for each achievement.

        ACHIEVEMENTS                SKILLS USED

1.

2.

3.

4.

3.    Identify and list the common skills used among the four achievements.

4.    How do your skills and experiences make you unique?
      As a communicator?

As a leader?


As a team member?


5.  Do your grades and attendance records reflect your real capabilities? If not, why not? What do the courses you've taken and the grade you've achieved tell about you, and what don't they reveal?


6.  Describe your desired lifestyle for a five-year span after your education is complete. What do you want to be doing 5 years from the time you graduate?


7.  What goals have you set and met in the past? Explain.


## Questions:

1.  How will your ability to discuss you special skills, interests, volunteer jobs, and leadership activities help you in a job interview?


2.  Which questions were most difficult to answer? Why?

## EXERCISE 14.7    QUESTIONING AT INTERVIEWS

**Purpose:**
1.     To help you prepare for the types of questions interviewers ask.

**Directions:**
1.     Imaging you are applying for a job in your chosen field.
2.     Answer the each type of question below.

Career Field Choice:    _____

1.     OPEN QUESTION:

       What attracted you to this business organization?

       _____

       _____

       _____

       _____

2.     CLOSED QUESTION:

       If you get the job, could you begin in a week?

       _____

       _____

       _____

3.     PROBING QUESTION:

       What makes you determined to pursue a career in _____ ?

       _____

       _____

       _____

       _____

4.     HYPOTHETICAL QUESTION:

Suppose your boss were away for a short-term disability and you were left in charge. How would you handle the personnel and the work?

_____

_____

_____

_____

## Questions:

1.     Which type of question was the most difficult to answer?  Why?

_____

_____

_____

2.     Why is thinking about the type of question you may have to answer an important part of preparing for a successful interview?

_____

_____

_____

(Adapted from Aurelius, R. H. & Verderber, R. F. (1995) *Instructor's Manual for Inter-Act: Using Interpersonal Communication Skills*. Belmont, CA: Wadsworth.

## EXERCISE 14.8    STRESSING THE IMPORTANCE OF COMMUNICATION

**Purpose:**
1.    To help you become aware of the emphasis from organizations and businesses on competent communication skills.

**Directions:**
1.    Find five advertisements for employment possibilities in three different newspapers: (1) your local paper, (2) a national paper such as *Wall Street Journal* or *Washington Post,* and (3) a paper from a major city other than the one in which you live.
2.    Identify the skills and experiences wanted by potential employers, especially notice the communication skills desired.

**Questions:**

1.    What skills are the employers looking for in new employees?

 

2.    What experiences are the employers looking for?

 

3.    What communication skills are requested by employers?

 

4.    What are the salary ranges for the jobs that you found advertised?

 

5.    How can you prepare for these job opportunities?

 

| | |
|---|---|
| Upward Communication | Downward Communication |
| Quid pro quo | Hostile Environment |
| Horizontal Communication | Outward Communication |
| Leadership | Task-oriented Leadership |
| Relationship-oriented Leadership | Authoritarian Leadership Style |
| Democratic Leadership Style | Laissez-faire Leadership Style |

| | |
|---|---|
| Communication in an organization that flows from superiors to subordinates. | Communication in an organization that flows from subordinates to superiors. |
| A type of sexual harassment that threatens an employee's rights through offensive working conditions or behavior on the part of other workers. | A Latin phrase for a type of sexual harassment. The phrase means "you do something for me and I'll do something for you." |
| Communication that flows to those outside an organization. | Communication among colleagues or co-workers at the same level within an organization. |
| A leadership approach that focuses on initiating work, providing information, and getting the job accomplished. | Behavior that influences, guides, controls, or inspires others to take action. |
| A leadership style that involves directing, giving orders, and seeking to control others. | A leadership approach that encourages others and maintains a supportive, friendly work climate. |
| A leadership style that involves minimal direction on the leader's part. | A leadership style that involves consulting workers and considering many points of view. |

| | |
|---|---|
| Situational Leadership Style | Interview |
| Open Question | Closed Question |
| Probing Question | Performance Review |
| Team | Journalist's Six Questions |
| Brainstorming | 6M Technique |
| Analyze Pros and Cons | Modem |

| | |
|---|---|
| A structured, planned discussion, usually between two people. | An approach to leadership that lets the situation and the needs of follows dictate the leadership style. |
| Type of interview question for which there is a more limited range of possible answers. | Type of interview question for which there is a wide range of possible answers. |
| An interview between an employee a supervisor designed to provide feedback about the employee's skills and abilities. | A question that an interviewer uses to seek more detailed information. |
| A technique for analyzing and defining issues by answering the question, who? what? where? when? why? and how? | A group of individuals organized to work together to achieve a common goal. |
| A method for structuring the analysis of a problem or issues by assessing manpower, machinery, methods, materials, money, and minutes. | A process of generating many ideas through free association separate from the process of evaluating the ideas. |
| Computing hardware that allows users to send and receive information via the phone line. | Simple technique for considering the advantages and disadvantages of a solution or proposal. |

| | |
|---|---|
| Scanner | Facsimile Machine |
| Interactive TV | Electronic Messaging (E-Mail) |

| | |
|---|---|
| Often called a fax, this machine transmits written documents over telephone lines. | A machine that permits you to insert photographs or text into a computer which you can then incorporate into documents and reports or send to others over phone lines. |
| A system that allows user's to generate and transmit messages via computer. | A television broadcasting system that allows users to communicate face-to-face over great distances. |